BUILD FIRST, MARKET LATER

The Engineer's Argument
for Breakthrough Innovation

Farhad Abtahi

2026
First Edition

DISCLAIMER

This book is a work of nonfiction intended for educational and informational purposes.

Historical examples, case studies, and quotations are presented based on publicly available sources and the author's best understanding at the time of writing. Some quotations are paraphrased or reflect commonly cited accounts; where attribution is uncertain or disputed, this is indicated in the text.

References to individuals, companies, or technologies are made in good faith and do not imply endorsement or criticism.

The analysis and opinions expressed represent the author's interpretation and do not constitute professional advice.

Trademarks mentioned in this book are the property of their respective owners.

DEDICATION

"There is a voice that doesn't use words. Listen."
Rumi (version by Coleman Barks)

To the engineers who build without permission,
persist without validation,
and trust their technical instincts over business orthodoxy.
You are building the future that the rest of us can't yet imagine.

THE ENGINEERING MIND

This book uses the word "engineer" not as a job title, but as a worldview. You know who you are. You are the one who cannot help but wonder how things work. You see systems where others see chaos. You build to understand, not just understand to build.

The Core Characteristics of the Engineering Mind

Systems Decomposition: You see the world as interconnected components that can be analyzed, modified, and improved.

First Principles Thinking: You are suspicious of "because we've always done it that way." You ask what physics allows, not what tradition dictates.

Building as Thinking: You understand through making, testing, breaking, and iterating.

Productive Obsession: You pursue problems beyond economic rationality simply because they must be solved.

This mindset ignores credentials. Michael Faraday began as an apprentice bookbinder. The Wright brothers were bicycle mechanics. Hedy Lamarr was an actress. They shared something more fundamental than a degree. They saw the world as something that could be shaped.

If you have ever lost yourself in solving a problem nobody asked you to solve, if you trust elegant solutions over market research, if you value what works over what sells, welcome.

You are among your people.

Who This Book Is For:

- Engineers and technical founders
- Platform and systems builders
- Deep-tech innovators
- Anyone building where feedback loops are slow, expensive, or nonexistent

Who This Book Is Not For:

- Incremental feature optimization
- Pitch-first entrepreneurship
- Short-cycle growth tactics

If you're optimizing a food delivery app or cloning an existing platform for a new niche, Lean methods work fine. This book is for the deep end of the pool.

A Note on Examples

The stories in this book are not intended as comprehensive histories. They are deliberately compressed accounts used to illustrate patterns of innovation, not to document every decision, debate, or contingency.

Innovation rarely unfolds in straight lines. What matters for the arguments in this book is not precise chronology, but sequence: what had to exist before something else could become possible. The examples are chosen and shaped to make those sequences visible.

A Note on What We Build: Invention vs. Innovation

Before we begin, we must dismantle a common barrier. The industry often tells you that unless you are discovering new physics (Invention), you aren't doing "real" engineering. Or conversely, that unless you are optimizing a business model (Innovation), you aren't creating value.

This book rejects that binary.

We use the Dediu Framework[1] to distinguish clearly: **Invention** is creating something new (such as the laser). **Innovation** is creating new value (eye surgery).

You do not always need an invention to create a breakthrough innovation. The iPhone contained no new physics, but it was a masterpiece of integration. AWS did not invent new computer science, but it was a masterpiece of architecture.

Whether you are discovering novel science (Deep Tech) or architecting novel systems (Platform Engineering), you are a **Builder**. This book grants you permission to build capability first, regardless of which category it falls into.

---

1. Dediu, H. (2014). Innoveracy: Misunderstanding Innovation. Asymco. (URL: https://asymco.com/2014/04/16/innoveracy-misunderstanding-innovation/)

The Central Paradox

There is a fundamental mismatch between how breakthrough innovations happen and how we are taught they should happen.

The dominant narrative screams: Identify problems. Validate with customers. Iterate quickly. Fail-fast.

This works brilliantly for incremental improvements. If you are building a better food delivery app, by all means, interview customers.

But transformative innovations, the kind that create new categories and change civilization, follow a different pattern entirely. They emerge from technical possibilities, not market requests. They require patient development, not rapid pivots. They demand builders who persist through years of skepticism, not entrepreneurs who pivot at the first sign of resistance.

The innovation establishment offers a false choice: follow their "Lean" methodologies or fail.

There is another way.

This book is not a new recipe. It is permission to break the existing ones. It is a defense of the engineering instinct to build first and market later.

TABLE OF CONTENTS

CHAPTER 1

THE STOCKHOLM QUESTION

"In silence, there is eloquence. Stop weaving and see how the pattern improves." — Rumi (version by Coleman Barks)

Stockholm's innovation ecosystem embraced me with the warmth of a thousand pitch competitions. It was 2013. I found myself sitting in converted warehouse spaces, surrounded by exposed brick and designer furniture, listening to yet another evangelist explain how design thinking and lean startup, when applied universally, would save the world.

But as I watched brilliant engineers dutifully filling out sticky notes for problems they had never experienced, a single question cut through the noise:

How can we actually make innovation happen? And why did this feel fundamentally wrong?

The Lean Canvas was our bible. Customer development, our salvation. "Get out of the building," they chanted, as if the hardest problems in physics, biology, or systems engineering could be discovered through coffee shop interviews rather than laboratories, workshops, and years of technical struggle.

What caught my attention was not the advice itself, but the fervor behind it. The prizes went to those with the best stories, not the best solutions.

I recall one particularly memorable competition where a team won an award for addressing challenges in cancer care. "Cancer is killing people," the presenter declared with the gravity of a state secret. The judges nodded sagely.

What went unquestioned was whether they had built or proposed any actual solution. It didn't matter that thousands of research groups were already working on oncology. It didn't matter that this team had no solution, no molecule, no mechanism of action. What mattered was the empathy map. They had interviewed five patients and "validated the problem."

Theranos was innovation theater at scale. They validated the problem, people hate blood draws, built empathy maps, secured prestigious partnerships, and raised over 700 million dollars. The pitch was flawless. The physics was impossible. They had validated everything except whether the technology worked.

This was innovation theater, an elaborate performance where everyone knew their lines, but nobody questioned the script.

Innovation Without Builders

Something subtle but dangerous has happened to innovation over the last two decades. It has been separated from the people who actually build things.

Innovation has become a function. A process. A department. A set of workshops and frameworks that can be discussed, analyzed, measured, benchmarked, and optimized. But in many organizations, it is no longer built.

This is innovation without builders.

Some have called this the "MBA-ification of innovation." The label is not important. The structure is. What matters is what happens when innovation is reduced to process, metrics, and risk management, and detached from technical ownership.

> *A reminder: as established in the Preface, "engineer" in this book means a worldview, not a credential. Business-minded founders who think in systems, question assumptions, and build to understand are, in this sense, engineers. The critique here targets organizational structure, not business education itself.*

In the innovation-without-builders model, innovation is managed rather than engineered. It is evaluated through slides instead of prototypes. Progress is tracked through KPIs instead of working systems. Risk is minimized before anything real exists. The work shifts from making something function in the world to explaining, justifying, and forecasting how it might function someday.

This did not happen by accident. It happened because innovation became something you could manage without building anything.

The result looks productive on paper. Roadmaps fill up. Funnels look healthy. Dashboards glow green. But nothing fundamental has changed.

Builders know something different.

For builders, innovation is not a process. It is a confrontation with reality. It is the moment when an idea meets physics, users, supply chains, regulations, edge cases, and failure. Builders learn by breaking things, fixing them, and discovering constraints no framework predicted.

When innovation is abstracted away from builders, those constraints disappear from decision-making. What remains are clean narratives, tidy pipelines, and optimism unburdened by implementation.

This is why so many organizations appear innovative while producing nothing new. They generate ideas faster than ever. They validate them with customers. They prototype them with AI. They iterate endlessly. But because no one is responsible for carrying an idea through years of technical friction, integration, and persistence, the work never crosses the threshold into reality.

Innovation without builders favors what is easy to explain over what is hard to build. It rewards clarity over correctness. It selects for ideas that fit existing structures rather than ideas that require new ones.

Incremental improvements thrive in this environment because they can be managed, measured, and optimized from a distance. Breakthroughs stall because they cannot. Breakthrough innovation demands deep technical ownership, long time horizons, and people willing to stay with a problem after the excitement fades.

AI accelerates this pattern. When ideas, prototypes, and analyses can be generated instantly, it becomes even easier to mistake activity for progress. The distance between decision-makers and builders grows wider, not smaller. Innovation becomes something you can simulate rather than something you must endure.

But real innovation has never worked that way.

If innovation feels harder today, it is not because the problems are smaller. It is because too much innovation is happening without builders. And without builders, innovation becomes theater.

The solution is not better frameworks or smarter metrics. It is restoring the builder to the center of innovation. Giving technical teams ownership, time, and authority. Accepting that real progress often looks slow, messy, and uncertain until suddenly it does not.

Innovation does not fail because organizations lack ideas. It fails because too few people are allowed, incentivized, and trusted to build them all the way to reality.

But look at the builders these ecosystems celebrate as successes. They did not follow the playbook.

Daniel Ek didn't validate Spotify through customer interviews; he saw that piracy was a superior user experience to iTunes and built a legal version that was faster than both.

The Collison brothers didn't use a Lean Canvas for Stripe; they saw developers struggling with payment integration and built the tool they wanted to use.

Elon Musk didn't pivot his way to reusable rockets through focus groups; he reasoned from first-principles about the cost of raw materials versus the cost of a ticket to orbit.

Oura's founders spent years building ring-form sensors without a clear mass market, only to have their killer application emerge during the COVID-19 pandemic. The market didn't validate the product; the product created the market.

The Recipe That Isn't

After attending dozens of these workshops, I realized a truth: We are teaching a recipe for innovation that the most successful innovators never followed.

It is as if we studied great chefs, noticed they all used salt, and concluded that salt was the secret ingredient, ignoring years of training, an understanding of chemistry, and an intuition for heat.

The standard recipe goes like this:

1. Identify a pain point.
2. Create an empathy map.

3. Build a Minimum Viable Product (MVP).
4. Test and pivot.

This works for the incremental, perhaps 70 percent of the problem space. But what happens when you are trying to create something genuinely new?

What customer could have told Tim Berners-Lee they needed the World Wide Web? What focus group would have requested CRISPR?

The Validation Trap

In these innovation workshops, the same question surfaced again and again: why did engineers seem resistant to the Lean Startup methodology?

The answer was simple. Because it doesn't work for breakthrough innovation.

Engineers understood this instinctively. The facilitators and evangelists reacted as if a law of nature had been challenged.

But that reaction reveals the deeper problem. The scientific method does not tell you which hypothesis to test. It does not tell you which mountain to climb.

The profound misdirection of current orthodoxy is the assumption that the market knows which mountains are worth climbing. It assumes customers can articulate needs for products that do not yet exist, for capabilities they cannot yet imagine.

The Failure Fallacy

"Fail fast, fail often."

This makes perfect sense when you are A/B testing a landing page. It is catastrophic when you are developing a fusion reactor.

Breakthrough innovation requires productive persistence: the ability to distinguish between a fundamental impossibility, like perpetual motion, and a hard problem that simply needs more work, like heavier-than-air flight.

James Dyson did not "fail fast." He built 5,127 prototypes. That was not a failure. It was the systematic exploration of a design space.

The problem with "fail fast" is not the idea of learning quickly. It is the assumption that feedback loops are instant. What if your innovation cannot be meaningfully measured for years? What if the infrastructure required to test it does not yet exist?

Google spent its early years refining its search technology long before search advertising became its dominant business model. Amazon reinvested heavily in retail and cloud infrastructure for many years before AWS became a major profit engine. Apple developed the first iPhone in relative secrecy over roughly three years before its 2007 launch.

In each case, early market feedback would have been not just unhelpful but actively misleading.

Systems Thinking in the Age of AI

A particularly striking aspect of our current moment is that just as large language models are making it possible to automate much of the surface-level innovation process, generating personas, pitch decks, and business plans, the real differentiator is becoming deep systems thinking. ChatGPT can write you a perfect Lean Canvas in seconds. It can generate hundreds of "validated" customer pain points. It can even create compelling pitch narratives. But it cannot do the deep technical work of understanding how systems interconnect, how changing one variable affects others, or how to reason from first principles about what is physically possible.

The rise of AI makes the engineering mindset more valuable, not less. When anyone can generate a plausible-sounding solution to almost any problem, the ability to distinguish between what sounds good and what actually works becomes crucial. The ability to think in systems, to understand feedback loops, emergence, and unintended consequences, becomes a core competency that AI cannot replicate.

Design thinking typically asks, "What do users need?" and optimizes toward better versions of existing things. Systems thinking asks, "What becomes possible?" and creates entirely new capabilities. This is not merely a methodological difference. It is an epistemological chasm that helps explain why designers excel at refining products, while engineers create new technological realities. Chapter 5 explores this distinction in depth.

The emergence of large language models themselves illustrates this pattern. No customer asked for them. No focus group validated the need. Instead, researchers at Google developed the transformer architecture in 2017 while attempting to solve a technical problem in machine translation: how to handle long-range dependencies in text. The breakthrough came from a technical insight, attention mechanisms, not from market demand. The applications that followed, from ChatGPT to GitHub Copilot, were discovered after the fact, not planned in advance.

The teams now succeeding with AI are not the ones using ChatGPT to fill out innovation canvases faster. They are the ones who understand the underlying systems well enough to see non-obvious applications. They understand the technology stack, from the logic of attention mechanisms to the emergent capabilities of scale. They think in systems, not stories.

The Success Stories Nobody Talks About

A revealing pattern emerges when examining how breakthrough innovations actually developed, especially those we now celebrate.

> *"Just doing a (free) operating system (just a hobby, won't be big and professional like GNU)." — Linus Torvalds*

Linux did not begin with a market analysis or a search for product-market fit. It began as a technical experiment that solved a problem its creator cared about. The ecosystem followed later.

Bitcoin followed a similar path. Satoshi Nakamoto did not start by interviewing people about their financial pain points. The white paper proposed a technical solution to the double-spending problem in distributed systems. Its applications, from a store of value to decentralized finance, emerged only after the system existed.

CRISPR was no different. Jennifer Doudna and Emmanuelle Charpentier were not responding to customer requests for gene-editing tools. They were studying bacterial immune systems. The therapeutic applications came years after the underlying mechanism was understood.

These are not exceptions. They are the rule for breakthrough innovation. Yet we continue teaching methodologies that assume markets can define problems before the underlying capabilities exist, approaches that would have rejected each of these ideas long before they had a chance to mature.

What They Teach vs. What Actually Happened

Innovation	What the Playbook Says	What Actually Happened	Time to Readiness*
Laser	Identify customer need upfront	A solution looking for a problem for decades	~20 years
Transistor	Start with user pain points	Bell Labs solving internal physics problems	Several years
ChatGPT /LLMs	Build MVP and iterate	Years of research before any mass user feedback	~5-6 years (2017-2022)
Linux	Find product-market fit	Started as a personal project solving a technical problem	Emergent
Bitcoin	Design thinking workshops	White paper solving double-spending without a market	~1-2 years to first use
CRISPR	Customer journey mapping	Fundamental biology research	5+ years
DeepMind	Validate product-market fit first	Research-first approach with unclear product	~4 years
iPhone	Focus groups and validation	Developed in secrecy, driven by vision	~2-3 years
Sony Walkman	Market research validation	Built despite market research skepticism	N/A

*This is an estimate of development timelines, not commercialization timelines

The Question That Matters

So, here's the question that started my journey toward writing this book: If the most successful innovations don't follow the innovation recipe we're teaching, why do we continue to teach it?

The answer has three parts:

First, these methodologies work well for incremental innovation, and most innovation is incremental. If you're building a marginally better CRM software or a slightly more efficient logistics platform, then yes, talk to customers, validate pain points, iterate based on feedback. The problem is we've universalized a specific tool into a general philosophy.

Second, the dominance of these methodologies isn't organic. It's structural. Venture capital firms need repeatable processes to evaluate hundreds of pitches. Accelerators need a curriculum they can teach in 12 weeks. Innovation consultants need frameworks they can sell to corporate clients. Lean Startup and Design Thinking provide exactly this: standardized, teachable, measurable processes that work for the incremental innovations most startups pursue.

The problem isn't that these methodologies exist. It's that the funding ecosystem has made them almost mandatory. When Sequoia, Y Combinator, Sting, and every accelerator from Stockholm to Singapore teach the same playbook, alternatives become invisible. Soft funding (grants, innovation funds, government programs) reinforces this by requiring customer validation and pivot readiness as prerequisites for funding. The entire financial infrastructure of innovation has crystallized around methodologies designed for incremental improvement.

This creates a selection bias: companies that succeed using customer-driven methods get funded and celebrated, while companies pursuing breakthrough innovation without customer validation struggle to raise capital. The ecosystem then points to its portfolio as evidence that customer-driven innovation works, ignoring that it's funding selection, not methodology superiority. As Peter Thiel observed, "Competition is for losers." But when the entire funding ecosystem pushes the same competitive playbook, heresy becomes financially risky.

To be clear: I'm not arguing these methodologies are wrong for all innovation. They're powerful tools for incremental innovation, which represents most of the innovation economy. My critique is that they've become the only acceptable approach, crowding out alternative paths that breakthrough innovation requires. When VCs demand pivot velocity, when accelerators require validated learning, when innovation grants mandate customer development, they're not optimizing for breakthrough; they're optimizing for predictability.

Third, and most insidiously, these methodologies shift power from builders to talkers. In a world where customer validation is king, the person who can articulate the problem becomes more valuable than the person who can solve it. MBAs matter more than PhDs. Pitch decks matter more than prototypes.

Beyond the Recipe

What I learned during my time in the innovation ecosystem, and what I've confirmed through years of observation and research since, is that innovation doesn't have a single recipe. At best, it has patterns, principles, and practices that increase the probability of a breakthrough in specific contexts. But for breakthrough innovation, these look different from the Lean Canvas or design thinking workshops that dominate today's landscape.

Real Breakthrough Innovation Often Looks Like:

Company/ Innovation	Duration	Key Characteristic
Bell Labs / Transistor	7 years	No customer validation
Dyson / Vacuum	5,127 prototypes	Funded by wife's teaching salary
Boston Dynamics / Robotics	29 years	Perfected locomotion before commercial product
Laser	20 years	No idea what it would be used for

None of these followed the standard innovation recipe. All of them changed the world.

The Nuance: When Methodologies Actually Help Breakthrough Innovation

Here's where critique must yield to nuance: Lean Startup and Design Thinking aren't categorically wrong for breakthrough innovation. They can be powerful tools when used selectively, with a proper understanding of their limitations.

Where these methodologies add value to breakthrough innovation:

Lean Startup can accelerate learning when you've already built the breakthrough capability and need to discover applications. Google used rapid iteration to discover AdWords as a business model after they'd built PageRank. The lean methodology helped them find the business model for an existing technical breakthrough.

Design Thinking can uncover latent needs that your breakthrough technology might address. IDEO's ethnographic methods can reveal workflow inefficiencies or emotional frustrations that technical founders might miss. The iPhone's breakthrough was technical, but its interface refinement benefited from an intense focus on usability. (Chapter 3 explores the limits of what customers can articulate about breakthrough innovations.)

Customer development can validate specific use cases once the technology exists. Qualcomm built CDMA first, then used customer feedback to prioritize which telecommunications applications to develop first. They weren't validating whether to build CDMA: they were validating which problems to solve with it.

The critical distinction: These methodologies work best as tools for refining and directing breakthrough innovations, not for discovering them. Use customer development to find applications for your technology, not to decide whether to build the technology. Use design thinking to make your breakthrough accessible, not to determine whether the breakthrough is worth pursuing. Use lean principles to accelerate learning about business models, not to decide whether the technical vision is valid.

The problem isn't the tools. It's the universalization. When these become the ONLY acceptable approach, when they're applied at the WRONG stage (before technical validation), when they're used to REPLACE rather than COMPLEMENT technical judgment, they become obstacles to breakthrough innovation.

Think of it this way: Design Thinking is excellent for making a rocket comfortable. It is terrible for deciding whether rockets should be reusable. Lean Startup is great for finding customers for a quantum computer, but it is useless for deciding how to build one. Customer development can help prioritize which disease to target with CRISPR, but it cannot tell you if gene editing is scientifically possible.

The methodologies aren't enemies. They're tools with specific use cases that we've mistakenly universalized.

The Engineer's Dilemma

This creates a profound dilemma for engineers and technical founders. The entire innovation ecosystem (from investors to accelerators to innovation consultants) expects you to speak the language of customer validation and rapid iteration. They want to see your empathy maps and pivot stories. But if you're working on genuine breakthrough innovation, these tools don't just fail to help: they actively hinder.

The result is a theater of compliance. Teams fabricate 3-year revenue roadmaps for technology that physics says is a decade away, just to satisfy a jury. Researchers abandon promising directions because they cannot articulate the "job to be done" in customer terms. And technical founders hire "business co-founders" whose primary skill might be translating technical reality into design-thinking fiction.

The saddest part? Many engineers have internalized this messaging. They genuinely believe they're somehow deficient for thinking in systems rather than stories, for trusting physics over focus groups, for building first and finding markets later. They've been taught that their natural inclinations (to understand deeply, to build carefully, to pursue technical excellence) are weaknesses to be overcome rather than strengths to be leveraged.

The Incomplete Map: What's Missing from the Debate

The inefficiency of the current system has created a new paradigm, sparking a debate between Lean Startup and Deep Tech. While important, this debate misses the bigger picture. Both frameworks see only part of the innovation landscape.

The Deep Tech movement emerged for good reason. Researchers studying quantum phenomena or developing novel materials couldn't validate customer needs through coffee shop interviews. They needed patient capital, long development cycles, and freedom to pursue technical possibilities without market pressure. The Deep Tech community correctly identified that Lean Startup orthodoxy was counterproductive for science-based innovation.

But in positioning itself as the alternative to Lean Startup, Deep Tech created its own orthodoxy: one that assumes innovation equals academic research plus patentable inventions plus capital-intensive R&D. This assumption creates blind spots as problematic as those it sought to correct.

The Platform Architecture Gap

When Jeff Bezos decided to open Amazon's internal infrastructure as AWS in 2006, he wasn't responding to customer validation. He was making an architectural insight: compute infrastructure could be abstracted, standardized, and offered as a service. This required building the complete architecture first; you can't iterate on a platform's API contracts and expect an ecosystem to emerge.

AWS doesn't fit the Lean Startup model (it's challenging to validate cloud infrastructure with early customers who are unaware of their need for it). It doesn't fit Deep Tech either (no patentable science, not from academic research, not capital-intensive R&D). Yet it created more value and enabled more innovation than most patentable inventions.

The same pattern appears in Arduino's hardware architecture, ROS's robotics middleware, and Kubernetes's container orchestration. These are architectural innovations: breakthrough insights about how systems should be structured. They create value through enabling ecosystems, not through patent portfolios.

The Open-source Strategy Gap

When Linus Torvalds released Linux in 1991 with "just doing a (free) operating system (just a hobby, won't be big and professional like gnu)," he violated every assumption of both frameworks. No customer validation. No patents. No capital. No academic credentials. No proprietary advantage. No business model.

Yet Linux now runs most of the internet, powers every Android phone, and dominates cloud infrastructure. TensorFlow, React, Kubernetes, and numerous other open-source projects follow a similar pattern: they succeed by giving away rather than protecting, by building ecosystems rather than products, and by leveraging network effects rather than IP barriers.

Neither Lean Startup (assumes proprietary advantage needed) nor Deep Tech (where investors treat patents as the only valid moat) can account for open-source as a strategic innovation approach. Yet some of the most transformative innovations of our era explicitly reject IP protection.

The Integration Complexity Gap

The iPhone contained no novel science. Every component existed before 2007: touchscreens, mobile processors, cellular radios, lithium batteries, and mobile internet. Apple didn't invent any of these. They integrated them in a way nobody else had imagined, with software, services, and design coherence that created a breakthrough product.

To a Deep Tech investor, this looks like a commodity play with no defensible hard science. To a Lean Startup practitioner, it looks like a risky "big bang" launch without piece-by-piece validation. Both frameworks would have rejected the most valuable product ever made.

Tesla follows the same pattern: battery technology from partners, electric motors that existed for a century, and software integration that nobody had attempted at this scale. The innovation wasn't in the components but in the radical integration of complex systems that established manufacturers thought impossible.

The three critical gaps (platform/architecture, open-source, and integration complexity) reveal a fundamental flaw in the current orthodoxy. Each framework fails because it measures innovation by a proxy metric rather than its true definition: **Utility driving Usage.**

- **Design Thinking fails** because it measures innovation by *articulated desire*. Users cannot articulate a utility they don't know is possible.
- **Lean Startup fails** because it measures innovation by *validation velocity*. You cannot iterate a platform foundation into existence; the utility only emerges once the complete system is built.
- **Deep Tech fails** because it measures innovation by *patentable invention*. It dismisses complex integration as "just engineering," ignoring that utility often comes from how components are combined, not just how they are invented.

By focusing on these proxies, the establishment misses the 'homeless' innovations, like Linux or the original iPhone integration, that generate massive utility and adoption without fitting the standard definitions of 'scientific invention' or 'validated product'.

The Complete Innovation Landscape

Match your innovation type to the right methodology

Innovation Type	Lean Startup?	Deep Tech?	The Gap / Best Approach	Examples
Software Incremental (features, A/B tests)	✓	✗	No gap—Lean works well	Facebook features, Spotify
Science-Based Deep Tech (physics, chemistry)	✗	✓	No gap—TRP works well	ASML, quantum computing
Platform/Architecture (infrastructure)	~	~	**CRITICAL GAP:** Ecosystem design + internal use first	AWS, Kubernetes, Arduino
Integration Breakthroughs (system complexity)	~	~	**CRITICAL GAP:** Systems thinking + vertical integration	iPhone, Tesla, SpaceX
Open Source Strategy (community-driven)	~	~	**CRITICAL GAP:** Community building + commercial layer	Linux, TensorFlow, React
Hardware Incremental (existing categories)	✓	✓	Both work—iterate with physical prototypes	Consumer electronics, IoT
Biotech/Pharma (regulatory-gated)	✗	✓	Regulatory-first, then market validation	Moderna, BioNTech

Legend: ✓ = Works well   ✗ = Poor fit   ~ = Partial/Neither   = CRITICAL GAP (this book's focus)

KEY INSIGHT: Most Breakthrough Innovations Fall in the Gaps

Platform, Integration, and Open Source innovations need different approaches—that's what this book provides.

From BUILD FIRST, MARKET LATER: The Engineer's Argument for Breakthrough Innovation

For detailed definitions of innovation types, invention vs. innovation, and the Dediu taxonomy that underlies this analysis, see Appendix A: The Complete Innovation Landscape

The Pattern Becomes Clear

Look at the previous table. The three critical gaps (platform/ architecture, open-source, and integration complexity) are characterized by common features that neither framework can accommodate:

- They can't be validated before building
  (violates Lean's requirement)
- They're not patentable science
  (violates Deep Tech's requirement)

- They emerge from engineering insight, not academic research
- They create moats through architecture/network effects, not IP protection
- They require patient, sequential development without market validation

Yet they represent some of the most transformative innovations of our era. They enable entire ecosystems of further innovation. They create categories rather than serving markets. They give builders leverage that individual products never achieve.

Why This Matters for Engineers

If you're building a platform, you might not be doing "Deep Tech" by conventional definition (no PhDs, no patents, no peer-reviewed publications). But you need the same "build first, market later" approach. You need patience to develop complete architectures before markets can evaluate them. You need technical excellence over customer validation.

If you're pursuing an open-source strategy, you're explicitly rejecting both frameworks' assumptions about IP protection and proprietary advantage. But you still need frameworks for building breakthrough innovations that markets don't yet understand.

If you're working on complex system integration, you might get dismissed by Deep Tech as "not innovative" (no novel science) while Lean tries to force you into iterative customer validation that destroys system coherence. But you're doing breakthrough engineering work that requires the same patient development and technical rigor.

The Real Issue: Orthodoxy Itself

The pattern reveals something deeper: the issue isn't "Deep Tech versus Shallow Tech." It's methodological orthodoxy preventing context-appropriate innovation.

Lean Startup orthodoxy says: "Everything can be customer-validated and rapidly iterated." This breaks for breakthrough innovations where customers can't imagine what you're building.

Deep Tech counter-orthodoxy says: "Only patentable, capital-intensive, science-based innovation needs different approaches." This breaks for architectural, open-source, and integration breakthroughs that require patient development without fitting Deep Tech's definition.

Both frameworks serve important contexts. Lean Startup works brilliantly for incremental software. Deep Tech correctly addresses science-based innovation. The problem lies in universalizing specific tools into general philosophies, thereby missing everything that falls outside both circles.

The Path Forward

What follows in this book is not another innovation recipe. I won't give you a new canvas to fill out or a certified methodology to follow. Instead, I'll show you how breakthrough innovation actually happens across the full spectrum (from science-based Deep Tech to architectural platforms to open-source ecosystems) using frameworks that match your context rather than forcing your innovation into orthodox categories.

We'll explore why technology-push innovation, despite being unfashionable, has created more transformative breakthroughs than all the customer development in the world. We'll examine how patient capital and technical excellence create more sustainable competitive advantages than first-mover advantage or network effects. We'll see why building without permission isn't just acceptable for breakthrough innovation. It's essential.

Most importantly, we'll develop frameworks that work with the engineering mindset rather than against it. Frameworks that leverage your ability to think in systems, to reason from first-principles, to pursue technical excellence even when the market doesn't yet understand what you're building. Whether you're working on patentable science, platform architecture, open-source strategy, or complex integration, this book provides context-appropriate guidance, not universal prescriptions.

In short, we'll reclaim innovation from the innovation consultants.

What Do You Think?

Have you sat through those same design thinking workshops, filled out those same canvases, and wondered why none of it felt quite right? Have you been told your technical vision needs more "customer validation" when customers can't even imagine what you're building?

Have you built architectural systems that couldn't be validated pre-build, platforms that required complete visions before anyone could understand their value?

Have you pursued open-source strategies that violated both frameworks' assumptions about IP protection and proprietary advantage?

Have you integrated complex systems in ways that weren't "innovative" by patent standards but transformed entire industries?

Does it resonate with you that we're using AI tools that violate every principle of customer-driven innovation to generate artifacts for customer-driven innovation processes?

Have you noticed that the engineers building the most transformative technologies (from quantum computers to brain-computer interfaces to cloud platforms) spend their time on technical challenges, not customer interviews?

If these questions resonate, if you've felt that disconnect between how innovation is taught and how breakthroughs actually happen, if your innovation doesn't fit neatly into either orthodox framework, then welcome. This book is for you.

Let's build first and market later.

But don't take my word for it. History provides the clearest evidence. Let's examine what actually happened when one of the 20th century's most transformative innovations emerged: an invention that created trillion-dollar industries despite having no customer demand, no validated market, and no clear application whatsoever.

References

1. Felin, T., Gambardella, A., Stern, S., & Zenger, T. (2019). "Lean Startup and the Business Model: Experimentation Revisited." Long Range Planning, 52(5), 101889.
2. Lizarelli, F. L., de Toledo, J. C., & Alliprandini, D. H. (2022). "Critical Success Factors and Challenges for Lean Startup: A Systematic Literature Review." The TQM Journal, 34(3), 534–551.
3. Morita, A., Reingold, E. M., & Shimomura, M. (1986). Made in Japan: Akio Morita and Sony. Dutton.
4. Thiel, P., & Masters, B. (2014). Zero to One: Notes on Startups, or How to Build the Future. Crown Business.
5. Ries, E. (2011). The Lean Startup. Crown Business.

CHAPTER 2

THE LASER LESSON

Like Benjamin Franklin[1] before him, Theodore Maiman could have asked a simple but prescient question in 1960: "What good is a newborn baby?" He had just invented the laser, and critics dismissed it as "a solution looking for a problem." This criticism should have been devastating. According to modern innovation theory, Maiman had committed the cardinal sin: building something nobody asked for.

Yet here's what makes the laser remarkable: it exemplifies exactly the pattern Chapter 1 described. Breakthrough innovation emerging from technical possibility, not market validation. The laser violated every rule of "smart" innovation. It took 20 years to find major applications. It required patient capital with no promise of returns. It emerged from pure physics research with no commercial intent. By every modern metric, it was a failure. By historical measure, it transformed civilization.

This matters because the laser's journey reveals fundamental flaws in how we think about innovation. The laser wasn't unique in this pattern. The transistor, GPS, the internet, and even the wheel

---

1. When skeptics in Paris questioned the utility of the Montgolfier brothers' hot air balloon demonstrations in 1783, Franklin reportedly replied, "What good is a newborn baby?", suggesting that nascent inventions, like infants, should be judged by their potential rather than their immediate usefulness.

were not solutions to problems that customers had articulated. They were possibilities that created their own necessities.

The Birth of a Solution Without a Problem

To understand the laser's significance, we need to return to Hughes Research Laboratories in Malibu, California, on May 16, 1960. Theodore Maiman, a physicist who'd been told by his advisor that masers (microwave amplification devices) were "a subject worked to death," had just achieved something his competitors at Bell Labs thought impossible: optical amplification using a ruby crystal.

The achievement was so unexpected that the journal Physical Review Letters rejected his paper as "just another maser paper." Nature published a brief 300-word summary. The world's response was essentially a shrug. The New York Times buried the announcement on page 46, between stories about local education board meetings and classified ads.

Particularly telling was Arthur Schawlow's reflection years later. Schawlow, who would win the Nobel Prize for laser spectroscopy, later reflected that having specific applications in mind might have constrained their thinking. This is not false modesty. It was recognition of a fundamental truth about breakthrough innovation. Having a specific application in mind would have constrained their thinking to existing paradigms.

The laser emerged from pure curiosity about quantum mechanics and light-matter interactions. Maiman wasn't solving a customer problem. He was exploring what physics made possible. The theoretical foundation came from Einstein's 1917 paper on stimulated emission (43 years before the first working laser). The journey from theoretical possibility to working device took nearly half a century. The journey from working device to widespread application would take another two decades.

Even the name reveals the backwards nature of its development. LASER (Light Amplification by Stimulated Emission of Radiation) describes what it does, not what problem it solves. Compare this to modern product names: PayPal (paying your pal), Uber (going über-quick), Airbnb (a bed, as if in air). These names signal solutions to problems. The laser just *was*.

The Twenty-Year Desert

What happened next should terrify anyone who believes in "fail-fast" methodology. For two decades, the laser wandered the desert of applications, searching for its promised land. This wasn't because engineers weren't trying. It was because the laser's possibilities exceeded imagination's boundaries.

The first proposed applications were almost comically wrong. The military imagined "death rays," a vision that consumed billions in research but never materialized beyond science fiction. The press called it "a death ray," "a science-fiction death ray," and my personal favorite from the Los Angeles Herald, "a beam that could kill at a thousand miles." These weren't applications; they were projections of cultural fears onto new technology.

Bell Labs, despite having lost the race to build the first laser, saw potential in communications. But the technology wasn't ready. Laser beams are scattered in the atmosphere, making free-space communication impractical. Fiber optics didn't yet exist in a form that could carry laser light efficiently. It would take until the 1970s for material science to catch up with photonics.

The medical community was slightly more prescient. Within a year of Maiman's invention, Columbia-Presbyterian Medical Center used a ruby laser for retinal surgery. But this was more of an experiment than an application. The laser was too powerful, too imprecise, too expensive. It would take years of engineering refinement before laser surgery became practical.

During these twenty years, the laser wasn't failing. It was evolving. Each "failed" application taught engineers something about light-matter interactions, about control systems, about materials. The death ray research led to an understanding of atmospheric propagation. The communication failures drove fiber optic development. The medical experiments revealed the need for different wavelengths, pulse durations, and power levels.

This is the opposite of pivoting. Modern innovation doctrine would have said: "Death rays didn't work? Pivot to something else. Are communications impractical? Find a different market. Are medical applications too expensive? Lower your costs or change your target."

But the laser pioneers didn't pivot: they persisted. They didn't change their solution to fit existing problems. They waited for the world to discover problems that only lasers could solve.

The Pattern Recognition

The laser's journey from "solution looking for a problem" to enabling technology of modern civilization isn't unique. It's the rule for breakthrough innovations. Consider these parallel journeys:

The Transistor (1947-1960s): When John Bardeen, Walter Brattain, and William Shockley invented the transistor at Bell Labs, they weren't responding to customer demand for smaller electronics. They were trying to create a solid-state replacement for vacuum tubes to improve telephone switching systems: an internal technical problem. The first commercial application? Hearing aids, in 1952. Not because customers asked for transistor-based hearing aids, but because that's where the technology's limitations (low power, high cost) were acceptable. It took over a decade before transistors revolutionized computing and consumer electronics.

Global Positioning System (1973-2000): GPS began as a military project to help submarines launch nuclear missiles accurately. No civilian asked for it. No market research suggested people wanted to know their location within meters anywhere on Earth. For its first two decades, GPS was a military-only system. Even after selective availability was removed in 2000, it took years for applications to emerge. Now? Everything from Uber to precision agriculture depends on GPS. The applications came after the capability, not before.

The Internet (1969-1995): ARPANET, the Internet's predecessor, was designed for resource sharing between research computers, not for social media, e-commerce, or streaming video. Tim Berners-Lee created the World Wide Web in 1989, not because customers demanded it, but because he wanted a better way to share information at CERN. Commercial internet service providers didn't emerge until the mid-1990s. Amazon was founded in 1994, 25 years after ARPANET's first message.

ID Quantique (Founded 2001): A contemporary example that echoes the laser's patience requirement. This quantum cryptography company, founded in 2001, took 18 years to become profitable. As CEO Grégoire Ribordy explains: "The traditional VC thinking of 'try and fail-fast' may make sense in some sectors, but it is out of place in the Deep Tech field. Certain technologies and markets take time to develop and mature." Their quantum key distribution technology found initial applications in Swiss elections and banking: uses nobody could have predicted when the company started. Deep Tech, Ribordy emphasizes, is "a marathon, not a sprint."

The pattern emerges clearly: breakthrough innovations create their own applications through a process of exploration and discovery, not through customer validation or market research.

The Innovation Timeline Nobody Wants to Hear

After studying dozens of breakthrough innovations, I've identified a consistent pattern that contradicts everything we teach about innovation timelines:

Phase 1: Theoretical Foundation (0-50 years before product)

Someone publishes a paper or discovers a principle that makes something theoretically possible. Einstein's 1917 paper on stimulated emission. Turing's 1936 paper on computation. Shannon's 1948 paper on information theory. These papers often predate practical application by decades.

Phase 2: Technical Demonstration (0-20 years)

Researchers prove it can be done, usually in laboratory conditions, with no concern for practical application. Maiman's laser. ENIAC. The Wright Flyer. Expensive, impractical, but proof that physics allows it.

Phase 3: Application Search (5-30 years)

The long, painful period where the technology searches for problems to solve. Most "failed" applications occur here. This is where VCs lose patience, where founders give up, where the media mocks the technology as overhyped.

Phase 4: Infrastructure Development (5-15 years)

Supporting technologies and systems emerge. For lasers: fiber optics, precision control systems, semiconductor lasers. For the internet: ISPs, web browsers, broadband. For electric vehicles: charging networks, battery technology.

Phase 5: Application Explosion (10-20 years)

Once infrastructure exists, applications multiply exponentially. Lasers go from curiosity to enabling everything from surgery to manufacturing to entertainment. The internet goes from a research tool to an economic foundation.

Phase 6: Invisible Ubiquity (ongoing)

The technology becomes so fundamental that we forget it exists. When did you last think about the lasers in your computer's optical drives, your fiber internet connection, your laser printer, and the barcode scanners at every store?

This timeline means that breakthrough innovations typically take 30-70 years from theoretical foundation to widespread adoption. That's not a bug. It's a feature. Complex technologies require time to mature, for complementary innovations to emerge, for society to reorganize around new possibilities.

Why Modern Frameworks Would Kill Breakthrough Innovation

Let's conduct a thought experiment. Imagine Theodore Maiman in 2024, trying to develop the laser using current innovation methodologies:

The Lean Startup Approach: Maiman creates a Lean Canvas. Customer Segments: Unknown. Problem: No specific problem. Solution: Coherent light beam. Unique Value Proposition: "Makes very pure light"? Revenue Streams: Unclear. He fails to validate any assumptions. VCs pass. Project dies.

Design Thinking Workshop: Facilitators run empathy mapping sessions. Users can't articulate needs for coherent light because they don't know what coherent light enables. The workshop pivots to "better flashlights" because that's a problem users can understand. The laser never happens.

Customer Development: Maiman interviews 100 potential customers. Industries mention vague desires: manufacturers want better cutting tools, doctors want precise surgical instruments, and telecommunications companies want higher bandwidth. But none specifically need lasers; they have working solutions. Without a clear customer pull, development stops.

Agile Development: Two-week sprints to show working software. But laser development requires months of precise crystal growing, careful optical alignment, and high-voltage power supplies. The PM demands visible progress every sprint. The team pivots to LED improvements: quicker wins, clearer applications.

Fail-Fast Philosophy: The first prototype doesn't achieve continuous operation. Only pulsed. "Failed" experiment. Pivot to something else. The second prototype is too expensive for any practical application. Another "failure." By prototype three, funding is pulled for lack of product-market fit.

The laser required what these methodologies can't provide: patience to explore without immediate applications, permission to build before validating markets, and trust that technical excellence would eventually find purpose.

Lean Startup is not wrong. It is incomplete. Its assumptions collapse when experiments are expensive, feedback loops are slow, and customers cannot articulate needs for capabilities that don't yet exist.

The Maser Mafia: How Solutions Create Their Own Ecosystems

A particularly fascinating aspect of the laser story is how the "solution looking for a problem" created an entire ecosystem of problem-finders. As the PayPal Mafia would later spawn multiple unicorns, the laser pioneers created a distributed network of innovation that found applications through exploration, not planning.

Charles Townes, who invented the maser (the laser's microwave predecessor), won the Nobel Prize not for solving a specific problem but for creating a tool that others used to solve problems he never imagined. His students and collaborators spread across industry and academia, each taking the core insight (stimulated emission could amplify electromagnetic radiation) and exploring different frequencies, materials, and configurations.

Gordon Gould, who coined the term "laser" and spent 30 years fighting for patent rights, had perhaps the clearest early vision of applications. His notebook from 1957 described uses in communications, spectroscopy, interferometry, and fusion. But even Gould's prescient vision missed the laser's biggest applications: optical storage (CDs, DVDs, Blu-ray), fiber optic internet, and barcode scanning. These applications required not just the laser but entire industries that didn't yet exist.

Bell Labs, despite losing the race to build the first laser, became the epicenter of laser applications. They had something crucial: patient capital and permission to explore. Researchers could spend years investigating laser properties without delivering quarterly results. This patience paid off. Bell Labs' laser research led to optical communications, which now carries 99% of intercontinental data traffic.

The significant realization: the laser's success came not from a single company or focused development effort but from a distributed, uncoordinated exploration of possibilities. No central planning committee decided lasers should be used for eye surgery, manufacturing, and telecommunications. Instead, thousands of researchers, engineers, and entrepreneurs each explored their corner of the possibility space.

The Lesson for Today's Engineers

So what does the laser lesson mean for engineers working on breakthrough innovations today? Several principles emerge:

First, embrace being a solution looking for a problem. If you've discovered something genuinely new (a material with unprecedented properties, an algorithm that solves previously intractable problems, a way to manipulate matter at new scales), don't apologize for not having clear applications. The applications will emerge through exploration.

Second, recognize that the timeline for breakthrough innovation is measured in decades, not quarters. If you're working on quantum computing, fusion energy, brain-computer interfaces, or any other fundamental technology, you're playing a long game. The pressure to show quick wins, to pivot rapidly, to fail-fast: this pressure is optimized for incremental innovation, not breakthrough discovery.

Katalin Karikó's mRNA Journey

Consider Katalin Karikó's mRNA journey: even longer than the laser's. In 1978, she began researching messenger RNA as a potential therapeutic platform. For 40 years, she faced rejection after rejection. The NIH declined her grant applications. The University of Pennsylvania demoted her from the tenure track in 1995 because her research wasn't attracting funding. Pharmaceutical companies showed no interest. The market-pull question ("Who will pay for this?") had no answer for four decades.

Then COVID-19 arrived. Karikó's mRNA research, accumulated across 45 years of patient persistence, became the foundation for both Pfizer-BioNTech and Moderna vaccines. In 2023, she won the Nobel Prize. The "solution looking for a problem" had found it, but only after the inventor persisted through demotion, funding rejection, and universal market indifference. No pivot. No fail-fast. Just 45 years of building capability until the world needed it.

Third, build for capabilities, not applications. The laser pioneers succeeded not by focusing on specific uses but by improving the fundamental capabilities of their devices: more power, different wavelengths, better control, and longer coherence. Each improvement opened new possibility spaces.

Fourth, create ecosystems, not just products. The laser's impact came from thousands of people exploring applications. If you've created a breakthrough technology, your job isn't just to find the killer app. It's to enable others to explore the possibility space.

Fifth, seek patient capital, not quick returns. Whether from government grants, corporate R&D budgets, or enlightened investors, breakthrough innovation requires funding sources that understand the decades-long timeline. The current VC model, with its 7-10 year fund lifecycle, is structurally incapable of supporting most breakthrough innovations.

The essential wisdom comes from Schawlow's observation: "We had no application in mind. If we had, it might have hampered us." Having specific applications in mind constrains thinking to existing paradigms. The laser's power came from exploring what coherent light made possible, not from solving predetermined problems.

The Questions That Matter

The laser's history suggests we're asking the wrong questions about breakthrough innovation.

Market-Pull vs Technology-Push Questions

Market-Pull Questions	Technology-Push Questions
What problem does this solve?	What becomes possible?
Who is the customer?	What constraints does this remove?
What's the business model?	What new behaviors might emerge?
How do we validate demand?	What infrastructure is needed?
When will this generate revenue?	What adjacent innovations might this enable?

The laser succeeded because its pioneers asked technology-push questions. They explored what became possible when you could generate coherent light, not what problems needed solving. This exploration revealed applications that no amount of customer discovery could have uncovered.

In Defense of Solutions Looking for Problems

The phrase "solution looking for a problem" is meant as criticism, implying wasted effort on unwanted technology. But the laser's history suggests we should embrace it as a badge of honor. The most transformative technologies are solutions that create their own problems, or rather, they reveal possibilities that redefine what we consider problems worth solving.

Before the laser, nobody considered the lack of precise surgical tools a pressing problem; surgeons worked with what they had. Before GPS, nobody considered not knowing their exact location a problem; maps and landmarks sufficed. Before the internet, nobody considered the inability to instantly access global information a problem; libraries and mail worked fine.

Corning's Gorilla Glass: 35 Years of Patience

Consider Corning's chemically-strengthened glass. In 1962, Corning developed an ion-exchange process called "Project Muscle" that replaced smaller sodium ions with larger potassium ions, creating damage-resistant glass. The technology found only niche applications (100 racing cars, some pharmaceutical vials) and was discontinued in 1971. For 35 years, the technology sat dormant, explicitly described by Corning executives as "a solution in search of a problem."

Then Steve Jobs called. Developing the iPhone in 2006, Jobs needed scratch-resistant glass that could survive pockets full of keys and coins. Corning's dormant technology was resurrected as "Gorilla Glass" and now protects over 8 billion devices worldwide. A more than 30-year gap between invention and application wasn't a failure; it was a solution waiting for its problem to emerge. Like the laser, Corning's glass created a new category of demand that couldn't have existed before touchscreen smartphones.

These technologies didn't solve problems: they created new realities where previous limitations became intolerable. They shifted our baseline expectations of what's possible. **This is the hallmark of breakthrough innovation: it doesn't satisfy existing demand but creates new categories of demand that couldn't have existed before.**

So when someone dismisses your work as "a solution looking for a problem," remember Theodore Maiman's response when asked about the laser's applications: "What good is a newborn baby?" Like a child, breakthrough innovations need time to grow, explore, and discover their purpose. The applications that matter most are rarely the ones imagined at birth.

Take it as a compliment. You're in good company. The laser looked for problems for twenty years. Gorilla Glass waited 34. The newborn that everyone dismissed grew up to power a trillion-dollar ecosystem.

The best innovations don't solve problems. They create possibilities.

The Blind Spot: When the Visionary Becomes the Skeptic

However, embracing these solutions is difficult because they often look awkward or unnecessary in the present moment. Ironically, even Steve Jobs, the man who had the vision to resurrect Gorilla Glass, fell into this exact trap regarding the size of the screen itself.

While Jobs saw the potential of the glass, he completely dismissed the "Large Screen" as a viable technology. He viewed the large displays of competitors not as innovation, but as a clumsy solution looking for a problem that didn't exist.

Jobs was right about biology but wrong about trajectory, a reminder that even visionaries can be trapped by present constraints.

Based on this observation, they identified the "Thumb Zone", the exact arc a human thumb can sweep across a surface without stretching. That measurement was roughly 3.5 inches diagonally.

For five years, this number was sacred. Jobs famously mocked larger phones as "Hummers", clunky solutions that nobody asked for. When a reporter asked him about the new wave of big Android phones, he scoffed: "You can't get your hand around it. No one's going to buy that."

To Jobs, the Large Screen was a failed solution because it broke the ergonomics of the thumb. He was right about the biology, but he was wrong about the horizon.

Creating the New Reality

Just as the laser created a world where we demanded precise light, the Large Screen created a world where we demanded mobile immersion.

By obsessing over how users *held* the phone (the existing problem), Apple missed why users were buying the competitors' "clunky" devices. Users were silently deciding that they didn't care about their thumbs anymore; they cared about their eyes. They wanted a pocket television, not just a phone.

The Large Screen was a solution that created a new problem: "How do I consume high-definition media on the bus?" Before the large screen existed, nobody thought asking that question was possible.

This is the danger of dismissing a "solution looking for a problem." You might be perfectly solving for the limitations of today (the thumb), while the "useless" technology is busy creating the possibilities of tomorrow (the eye). The best innovations don't just fit the hand we have; they force us to let go and reach for something else.

References

1. Ribordy, G. (2019). "The 'Try and Fail-Fast' Mentality Is Out of Place in Deep Tech." StartupTicker.ch, November 2019.
2. Maiman, T. H. (1960). "Stimulated Optical Radiation in Ruby." Nature, 187(4736), 493–494.
3. Townes, C. H. (1999). How the Laser Happened: Adventures of a Scientist. Oxford University Press.
4. Hecht, J. (2005). Beam: The Race to Make the Laser. Oxford University Press.
5. Karikó, K. (2023). "Nobel Prize Lecture." Nobel Foundation.

CHAPTER 3

IMAGINATION BOUNDARIES

If Steve Jobs, the greatest product visionary of our time, could miss the future of the smartphone because of rigid views on ergonomics, he's in good company. History shows that inventors are often the last to recognize what they've actually created.

We can call this the *Intended Use Fallacy*.

The Intended Use Fallacy is the dangerous belief that a technology's value is defined by the problem its inventor intended to solve. When you create a solution looking for a problem, you have a specific problem in mind. But often, that vision is a mirage, and the real opportunity lies in a direction you're actively ignoring.

Edison's "Serious" Machine

Consider Thomas Edison and the phonograph. When Edison invented it in 1877, he had created a miracle: a machine that could capture and replay the human voice. A solution of distinct genius.

But what was the problem?

Edison was a pragmatic man. To him, the answer was obvious: business efficiency. He published a list of ten potential uses. At the top: "Letter writing and all kinds of dictation without the aid of a stenographer," "Phonographic books," and "The teaching of elocution."

Music was on the list, but only as a low priority.

When entrepreneurs began buying phonographs to create coin-operated jukeboxes for entertainment arcades, Edison was *offended.* He complained that his serious office machine was being "debased into a toy." He resisted the pivot to entertainment for years, insisting the device was meant for serious work: capturing the dying words of great men, or office dictation.

He suffered from the same blindness as Jobs.

- Jobs thought the iPhone was a **Communications Tool** (governed by the thumb).
- Edison thought the Phonograph was a **Productivity Tool** (governed by the office).

Both were obsessed with *utility.* The market was obsessed with *experience.* The public didn't want to dictate memos; they wanted to listen to Mozart. The "problem" the phonograph actually solved wasn't stenographer inefficiency. It was the ephemeral nature of music.

> *"A lot of times, people don't know what they want until you show it to them."* **Steve Jobs**

This isn't a failure of market research; it's a fundamental cognitive limitation that no amount of empathy mapping can overcome.

Humans think in variations of what exists, not in what could exist. We request faster horses, not automobiles. Better typewriters, not word processors. Clearer phone calls, not video conferences. This isn't a failure of creativity. It's how cognition works. Our brains are prediction machines trained on past data. Asking customers to envision breakthrough innovation is like asking a fish to describe flight.

Yet the entire customer development movement, from Steve Blank's *Four Steps* to Eric Ries's *Lean Startup*, is predicated on the belief that customers hold the keys to innovation. "Get out of the building," they chant. "There are no facts inside your building, only opinions."

But what if the facts outside the building are constrained by the same cognitive boundaries that limit imagination inside it?

The Xerox Copier: A Case Study in Customer Blindness

In 1959, Haloid Xerox (later Xerox Corporation) faced a crisis that should be taught in every innovation course. They had spent over a decade and tens of millions of dollars developing the 914 copier: the first automatic plain-paper copier. When they hired Arthur D. Little, the gold standard of consulting firms, to conduct market research, the results were devastating.

The consultants interviewed potential customers across industries. The feedback was unanimous: nobody wanted it. The 914 was too big (the size of two washing machines), too expensive ($29,500 in today's dollars), and solved a problem customers didn't know they had. Companies were satisfied with carbon paper and mimeograph machines. The Arthur D. Little report concluded that Xerox might sell 5,000 units total. Ever. They recommended abandoning the project.

The particularly revealing aspect was the methodology. Arthur D. Little did everything right by modern standards. They interviewed hundreds of potential users. They analyzed existing copying methods. They calculated ROI based on current copying volumes. They validated (or rather, failed to validate) every assumption. Their research was thorough, professional, and completely wrong.

Xerox ignored them. By 1965, revenues hit $500 million. By 1966, over 200,000 units were in operation. The 914 became one of the most successful industrial product launches in American history. How did the world's best consultants get it so wrong?

The answer reveals the fundamental flaw in customer development: customers evaluated the 914 based on their existing copying needs (perhaps a dozen copies a day). They couldn't imagine how a fast, high-quality copier would change behavior. Once the 914 arrived, copying exploded from dozens to thousands of pages daily. **The machine didn't serve existing demand; it created new behavior.**

This pattern repeated decades later when Xerox's Palo Alto Research Center (PARC) invented the graphical user interface, the mouse, and networked computing. When they showed these innovations to corporate customers and even Xerox's own executives, the response was confusion and disinterest. Customers wanted faster terminals, not windows and icons. Steve Jobs saw what customers couldn't, not because he was a visionary, but because he wasn't constrained by what customers said they wanted.

The iPhone Focus Groups That Never Happened

The mythology around the iPhone includes a revealing absence: there were no focus groups. No customer development. No validated learning. The iPad followed the same philosophy, one Jobs had articulated years earlier: "It's really hard to design products by focus groups. A lot of times, people don't know what they want until you show it to them." This conviction ran deep. When developing the Mac, Jobs had stated, "We didn't build Mac for anybody else. We built it for ourselves. We were the group of people who were going to judge whether it was great or not."

Let's imagine, for a moment, if Apple had conducted customer development for the iPhone in 2005:

Moderator: "We're thinking about making a phone with no physical keyboard. All typing would be on glass."

Customer 1: "That's insane. I need to feel the keys. What about typing without looking?"

Customer 2: "BlackBerry has perfected the keyboard. Why would I want worse typing?"

Moderator: "It would have a 3.5-inch screen and cost $599."

Customer 3: "My laptop cost $599! For a phone? The Motorola RAZR is $200 and fits in my pocket."

Moderator: "The battery would last about a day with normal use."

Customer 4: "My Nokia lasts a week! This is going backwards."

Moderator: "But you could browse the real internet, not just WAP sites."

Customer 5: "I have a computer for that. I just need a phone that makes calls and does email."

Every piece of customer feedback would have killed the iPhone. RIM's co-CEO Mike Lazaridis perfectly captured the customer development view when the iPhone launched, acknowledging Apple's talent while noting the device's weak battery life and questionable keyboard. He was evaluating the iPhone against what customers currently valued. By those metrics, the iPhone was inferior.

What customers couldn't articulate was that they'd value different things once those things existed. They couldn't say "I want to carry the entire internet in my pocket" because that wasn't a conceptual possibility. They couldn't request apps because the very concept of a mobile app store didn't exist. They couldn't ask for a device that would replace their camera, GPS, iPod, and eventually their wallet because they didn't see these as one device.

The iPhone succeeded not despite ignoring customers but because it ignored them. It didn't satisfy articulated needs. It created new needs by changing what was possible. Within a decade, the question changed from "Why would I want that?" to "How did we live without this?"

The Faster Horse Problem (And Why It's Deeper Than You Think)

The famous quote attributed to Henry Ford ("If I had asked people what they wanted, they would have said faster horses") has become a cliché. Though likely apocryphal (no contemporary source exists, and the Henry Ford Museum has no record of him saying it), the sentiment captures a real cognitive limitation worth examining. The quote is often dismissed as elitist. But whoever originated it was describing a fundamental constraint of human imagination.

When we think about improvements, we think in terms of attributes of existing solutions:

Existing Solution	Imagined Improvement
Horses	Faster horses
Candles	Brighter candles
Ice delivery	More frequent ice delivery
Telegraphs	Longer-distance telegraphs
Typewriters	Electric typewriters

Customers can imagine quantitative improvements (faster, brighter, more, longer) but struggle with qualitative shifts (internal combustion, electricity, refrigeration, telephone, word processing). This isn't stupidity. It's how our brains process information. We use existing categories to understand new information. When those categories don't exist, comprehension fails.

What a Customer in 1900 Would Need to Imagine to Request an Automobile

#	Required Infrastructure	Status in 1900
1	Internal combustion engines	Not yet reliable
2	Petroleum infrastructure	Not yet built
3	Paved roads	Not yet common
4	Traffic laws	Not yet invented
5	Parking systems	Not yet needed
6	City reorganization around cars	Unimaginable

The automobile wasn't just "faster transportation." It was a system that required reimagining civilization. No customer interview could have revealed this because customers think in terms of their current system, not in terms of systems that don't yet exist.

This cognitive limitation extends beyond physical products. Before Facebook, nobody requested "a platform to share my life with hundreds of acquaintances." Before Google, nobody asked for "instant access to all human knowledge." Before Bitcoin, nobody demanded "trustless peer-to-peer digital currency." These weren't latent needs waiting to be discovered through careful customer research. They were impossibilities that became necessities only after they existed.

Clayton Christensen captured this paradox in his disruption theory: "The innovator's dilemma reveals that successful companies fail precisely because they serve their existing customers too well." His principle (find people for products, not products for people) acknowledges that breakthrough innovations create their own markets rather than serving existing ones.

Consider large language models. The market did not fail to imagine large language models. It was structurally incapable of requesting them. No focus group in 2015 said, "I want a model trained on the entire internet that can write like a human." The capability had to exist before the demand could form.

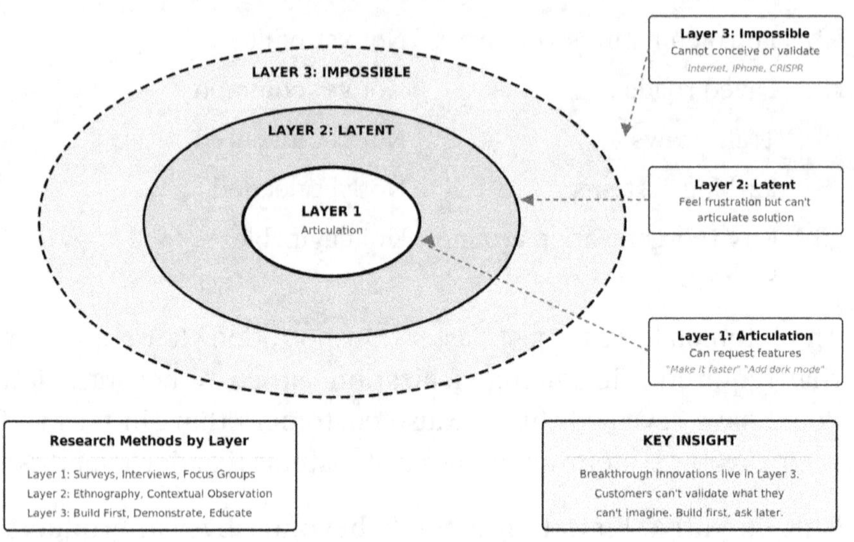

Every innovation methodology carries implicit assumptions about what customers can tell you. Lean assumes customers can validate certain hypotheses. Design thinking assumes customers can articulate frustrations. Jobs-to-be-Done assumes customers can describe the job they are trying to accomplish.

These assumptions hold—until they don't.

The failure modes of modern innovation all begin at this boundary.

I have synthesized these limits into what I call the Customer Imagination Boundary Model, four distinct zones of customer cognition, and the methods appropriate to each.

Layer 1: The Articulation Zone (What Customers Can Request)

- Incremental improvements: Faster, cheaper, smaller, more
- Feature additions: "It would be nice if it also…"
- Pain point solutions: Fixing obvious frustrations with existing products
- Aesthetic preferences: Colors, styles, interfaces

This is where customer development excels. If you're building version 2.0 of anything, customers provide invaluable feedback.

Layer 2: The Latent Zone (What Customers Feel But Can't Articulate)

- Emotional frustrations: "Something feels wrong, but I can't explain what."
- Workflow inefficiencies: Problems they've adapted to and no longer consciously notice
- Social needs: Status, belonging, identity expression, they won't admit

This is where skilled ethnographic research can reveal insights. Watch what customers do, not what they say. But even here, you're discovering problems within existing paradigms.

Layer 3: The Impossible Zone (What Customers Cannot Conceive)

- Category-creating products: Personal computers, smartphones, social networks
- Paradigm shifts: From ownership to access, from physical to digital, from synchronous to asynchronous
- Behavior changes: New habits that will only emerge after the technology exists
- System-level transformations: How innovation reshapes society, economics, culture

This is where customer development fails completely. No amount of customer research would have predicted teenagers spending eight hours daily on smartphones because the behavior didn't exist to be observed.

Layer 4: The Physics Zone (What Becomes Possible Through Technical Advance)

- New capabilities: Quantum computing, brain-computer interfaces, fusion energy
- Constraint removal: What happens when fundamental limitations disappear
- Emergent properties: Behaviors that arise from scale and network effects

This is the realm of technology-push innovation. Engineers explore what physics allows, not what customers request.

Innovations move through these layers over time. The iPhone started in Layer 4 (what touchscreens and miniaturization made possible), created Layer 3 changes (new behaviors and categories), eventually became Layer 2 (latent frustrations with current phones), and now lives in Layer 1 (customers can articulate exactly what they want in the next iPhone).

Why Ethnography Fails at the Frontier

The innovation establishment, confronted with the failure of direct customer questioning, pivoted to ethnography. "Don't ask customers what they want," they now say. "Observe them in their natural habitat. Uncover unarticulated needs through deep observation."

IDEO popularized this approach, and design thinking workshops worldwide now teach ethnographic methods. The logic seems sound: if customers can't tell you what they need, watch them struggle and innovate around their struggles.

But ethnography has the same fundamental limitation as customer interviews: you can only observe behaviors that exist. You can't observe someone struggling with the absence of something they can't imagine.

Consider some ethnographic studies that would have failed:

- **1995:** Observing people shop would not have revealed the need for e-commerce. Nobody was struggling with the inability to shop from their couch at 2 AM.
- **1999:** Watching music listeners would not have predicted Spotify. People weren't frustrated by owning music; they were proud of their CD collections.
- **2003:** Studying social interactions would not have revealed Facebook. People weren't struggling to broadcast their lives to hundreds of acquaintances.

The anthropologist Claude Lévi-Strauss called this "bricolage": making do with what's at hand. Users are brilliant bricoleurs, creating workarounds and adaptations. But these adaptations reveal how to better serve the existing paradigm, not how to transcend it. Watching people sharpen their typewriter ribbons wouldn't have led to word processing. Observing telegraph operators wouldn't have revealed the telephone.

The ethnography movement is customer development in disguise: a more sophisticated version of the same flawed premise that users hold the keys to breakthrough innovation. They don't. They can't. The cognitive boundaries that limit what customers can request also limit what ethnographers can observe.

The Horseless Carriage Syndrome

Innovation	Transitional Name	Conceptual Anchor
Automobile	Horseless carriage	Horse-drawn carriage
Television	Radio with pictures	Radio
Personal Computer	Electronic typewriter	Typewriter
E-mail	Electronic mail	Postal mail
Smartphone	Computer phone	Phone + Computer
E-books	Digital books	Physical books

These transitional names represent conceptual bridges between old and new paradigms. They're necessary because human cognition requires familiar anchors to understand unfamiliar concepts. But they also constrain thinking about what's possible.

When the automobile was a "horseless carriage," inventors put the engine where the horse would be and designed the cabin like a carriage. It took decades to realize that automotive design could be fundamentally different from carriage design. The conceptual baggage of "horseless" limited innovation.

Similarly, early television was conceived as "radio with pictures," leading to filmed radio shows. It took years to discover television's unique grammar: multiple camera angles, visual storytelling, and the power of the close-up. The medium's potential was constrained by its description.

Breakthrough innovations eventually shed these transitional names. Nobody calls cars "horseless carriages" anymore. We don't say "electronic mail"; we just say email. The transition from metaphorical to literal naming marks the innovation's maturity and society's cognitive adaptation.

Building for the Unimagined Future

If customers can't request revolutions, how should engineers approach breakthrough innovation? The answer requires abandoning customer-centric thinking for possibility-centric thinking. As Anthony Ulwick argues in his outcome-driven innovation framework, the focus should shift from what customers say they want to what outcomes would transform their reality.

Alternative Questions for Breakthrough Innovation

Instead of Asking...	Ask...
What problems do users have?	What constraints can we remove?
How can we improve this?	What if this assumption wasn't true?
What would users pay for?	What becomes possible?

These questions lead to different answers. When Elon Musk approached rockets, he didn't ask customers what they wanted from space travel. He asked why rockets cost so much. When he discovered they were thrown away after each use, he asked why we couldn't land and reuse them. Physics said it was possible. Customers (including NASA) said it was unnecessary.

When Jennifer Doudna and Emmanuelle Charpentier developed CRISPR, they weren't responding to pharmaceutical company requests for better gene editing. They were studying how bacteria fight viruses. The application to human gene editing came later, after the capability existed.

When Satoshi Nakamoto created Bitcoin, no customer was asking for a decentralized digital currency. People weren't sitting around frustrated by the inability to transfer value without intermediaries. The capability created the demand, not vice versa.

The greatest value comes from building things customers can't

request. This requires accepting that you'll be misunderstood, that you won't have customer validation, that smart people will explain why nobody wants what you're building. It requires the courage to trust technical insight over market research.

The Freedom of Building Without Permission

The customer development movement has created a permission structure where innovators need customer validation before building. This makes sense for incremental innovation: why build something nobody wants? But for breakthrough innovation, waiting for customer permission is waiting forever.

Customers can't give you permission to build something they can't imagine. They can't validate solutions to problems they don't know exist. They can't request revolutions because revolutions require imagining different systems, not better components within existing systems.

The Winner's Curse: When Pitch Validation Fails

But let me be clear about what "build without validation" doesn't mean. It doesn't mean that winning pitch competitions or getting external acclaim validates your product. Consider Meeshkan, winner of Slush 2018, one of Europe's most prestigious startup competitions. They developed sophisticated machine learning testing tools that wowed judges with technical elegance. They raised €370,000 in pre-seed funding. The innovation establishment declared them winners.

Then reality intervened. Despite the trophy, despite the funding, despite the expert validation, Meeshkan struggled to find product-market fit. They pivoted from their original ML training tools to API testing, launched on various platforms seeking traction, but eventually ceased operations. The technology was genuinely advanced, but the market wasn't ready (or perhaps the product-market fit gap was never going to close, regardless of pivot attempts).

The lesson isn't that Meeshkan should have done more customer validation. The lesson is that pitch validation is theater, too. Competition judges evaluate presentation quality, technical sophistication, and market narrative. They can't evaluate whether customers will actually pay. As one longitudinal study of competition winners from 2020-2025 concluded: "Competition success is a leading indicator of pitch polish, but not necessarily of operational durability or product-market fit."

This is the Winner's Curse: the hype generated by external validation can mask underlying business model flaws, creating pressure to execute the vision pitched on stage rather than the vision the market actually needs. Building without customer validation doesn't mean building without reality checks. It means the reality check comes from physics, from technical feasibility, from whether the thing actually works, not from whether audiences applaud.

Bootstrap Discipline vs. VC Cushion

There's a harder question worth asking: Would Meeshkan's trajectory have been different with a bootstrap approach? We can never know for certain (counterfactuals are comfortable that way). But the logic deserves examination.

Bootstrapping imposes a discipline that VC funding removes: the need for paying customers early. Without €370,000 in runway, the team would have been forced to find someone willing to pay for their tools within months, not years. That pressure might have revealed the product-market fit gap faster or forced a pivot toward where actual demand existed. The Slush trophy and the funding created breathing room that felt like validation but may have been a cushion against reality.

More fundamentally, bootstrapping means running with

minimal burn rate, which buys something invaluable: time to find serendipitous luck. The startup graveyard is filled with companies that ran out of runway six months before their market materialized. When you're burning €30,000 per month, you have a fixed number of lottery tickets. When you're burning €3,000 per month, you can wait for the market to come to you, pivot repeatedly, or stumble into adjacent opportunities that VC timelines would never permit.

This connects to a pattern I've observed repeatedly: VC funding can delay the reckoning that bootstrapping forces immediately. When customers fund you, every month is a referendum on whether you're building something valuable. When investors fund you, you can mistake runway for progress. The constraints of bootstrapping aren't just financial; they're epistemic. They force you to learn what the market actually wants rather than what judges think it should want.

This isn't an argument for arrogance or building in isolation. It's an argument for recognizing the fundamental cognitive constraints that limit what customer development can reveal. Customers are experts on their current reality, but cannot be experts on realities that don't yet exist.

The most liberating insight for engineers is this: for breakthrough innovation, customer ignorance isn't a bug. It's a feature. It means there's no competition. Nobody else is building it because nobody is asking for it. The very fact that customers can't request it is what makes it valuable.

So when someone asks, "But what customer wants this?" remember that's often the wrong question. The right question is: "What becomes possible?" In the gap between what customers can imagine and what physics allows lies the opportunity for breakthrough innovation.

If customers can't guide breakthrough innovation, what can?

Engineers have always known the answer: start with physics. Strip away accumulated assumptions and rebuild from fundamental reality.

References

1. Christensen, C. M. (1997). The Innovator's Dilemma: When New Technologies Cause Great Firms to Fail. Harvard Business Review Press.
2. Isaacson, W. (2011). Steve Jobs. Simon & Schuster.
3. Ulwick, A. W. (2005). What Customers Want: Using Outcome-Driven Innovation to Create Breakthrough Products and Services. McGraw-Hill.
4. Blank, S. (2013). The Four Steps to the Epiphany. K&S Ranch.
5. Ries, E. (2011). The Lean Startup. Crown Business.

CHAPTER 4

FIRST PRINCIPLES THINKING

What's the raw material cost of a rocket?

A s Musk would later explain: "I think it's important to reason from first-principles rather than by analogy". The normal way we conduct our lives is we reason by analogy. We are doing this because it's like something else that was done. It's mentally easier to reason by analogy rather than from first-principles. First principles are kind of a physics way of looking at the world. You boil things down to the most fundamental truths and say, 'What are we sure is true?' and then reason up from there."

First principles thinking is the engineer's superpower. It's the ability to strip away accumulated assumptions and rebuild from physical reality. While others ask, "How has this been done?" engineers ask, "What do the laws of physics actually allow?"

This isn't just a different methodology; it's a different epistemology. Market-pull innovation accepts the world's current configuration as given and asks how to optimize within it. First principles thinking questions whether that configuration needs to exist at all. Engineers create breakthrough innovations while consultants create incremental improvements because engineers can see past human conventions to physical possibilities.

The Physics Filter: What's Actually Impossible?

When James Dyson started developing his vacuum cleaner in 1978, every expert knew that vacuum cleaners needed bags. This wasn't opinion; it was an engineering fact. The bag served three functions: it collected dirt, it filtered air, and its growing resistance as it filled helped protect the motor from overheating. Removing the bag meant solving all three problems simultaneously.

Dyson asked a different question: what does physics require? Physics requires separating particles from the air. It doesn't require bags. In sawmills, he'd seen cyclonic separators remove sawdust from the air using centrifugal force. Physics said the same principle could work at the household scale. Industry experts said he was wrong.

Dyson built 5,127 prototypes over five years. This wasn't random iteration or "failing fast." Each prototype tested a specific hypothesis about airflow, cone angles, or particle separation. He was mapping the actual physics, not the industry's assumptions about physics. When he finally launched, his vacuum didn't just lack a bag. It fundamentally reimagined how household cyclonic separation could work.

Iteration is not the same as abandoning a hypothesis. Dyson explored the design space exhaustively without pivoting away from the core problem. Each prototype tested cyclonic separation; he never pivoted to "better bags" because customers preferred familiarity.

The Physics Filter in Action

Domain	Industry Assumption	First Principles Question	Result
Rockets	Expendable (reuse impossible)	Does physics prevent reuse?	No, just engineering
Batteries	Too expensive at $600/kWh	What do raw materials cost?	$80/kWh; supply chain gap
Lithography	Multiple competitors exist	What does physics require?	ASML 90% monopoly
Supersonic	Economically impossible	Physics or 1960s tech?	Modern materials change it
Grid Storage	Requires lithium-ion	What does physics actually require?	Iron-air batteries: 95% cost reduction

Rockets: Everyone knew rockets were expendable because the stresses of launch and reentry made reuse impossible. Musk asked: Does physics prevent rocket reuse? No. Physics makes it hard, not impossible. The issue was engineering and economics, not fundamental laws.

Batteries: The auto industry knew electric cars couldn't work because batteries were too expensive at $600/kWh. Musk asked: What do lithium, cobalt, and graphite actually cost? About $80/kWh. The gap wasn't physics; it was supply chain and manufacturing assumptions.

Lithography: The semiconductor industry believed multiple companies would compete in extreme ultraviolet (EUV) lithography. ASML asked: What does physics require for sub-10nm chips? The answer: light sources so complex that only one company could justify the R&D. Today, ASML holds a 90% monopoly on EUV lithography machines, each costing $200 million, because they understood the physics better than anyone else.

Supersonic Flight: After Concorde's commercial failure, everyone knew supersonic passenger flight was economically impossible. Boom Supersonic asked: Was it physics or 1960s technology? Modern materials, engines, and computational fluid dynamics change the equation entirely.

Grid Storage: Everyone knew grid-scale energy storage required lithium-ion batteries (expensive, resource-constrained, limited duration). Form Energy asked: What does physics actually require? Their answer: reversible rusting. Iron-air batteries breathe oxygen to rust iron when discharging, then reverse the process when charging. The chemistry was demonstrated in the 1970s by Westinghouse but abandoned. Form Energy's first-principles insight: iron is cheap and abundant, oxygen is free, and grid storage doesn't need lithium's energy density since the batteries don't need to move.

First principles thinking often reveals that "impossible" is actually "difficult," "expensive," or "we've always done it differently." The physics filter removes all of these false constraints, leaving only actual physical laws: conservation of energy, thermodynamics, and speed of light. **Everything else is negotiable.**

The Assumption Stack: Why Industries Can't Think

Every industry operates on what I call an "assumption stack": layers of accepted truths that become invisible through repetition. These aren't lies; they're simplifications that made sense at some point but calcified into unquestionable doctrine. The deeper the assumption in the stack, the harder it is to question.

The Automotive Assumption Stack (Before Tesla)

Layer	Difficulty to Question	Assumptions
Surface Layer	Easier	Dashboards need physical buttons; Dealerships handle sales
Middle Layer	Harder	Cars need model years; Service generates profit; Engines require maintenance
Deep Layer	Nearly Impossible	Cars must be personally owned; Refueling takes minutes; Performance requires engine noise
Foundation Layer	Invisible	Transportation requires burning something; Cars are mechanical systems; Complexity equals capability

Tesla questioned every layer. No dealerships. No model years. No engine maintenance. No ownership required (via software-limitcd battcry packs). No burning anything. Cars as computers. Simplicity as sophistication.

Established companies can't question deep assumptions because their entire infrastructure depends on them. Ford can't question dealerships; they have contracts. BMW can't question engine noise; it's their brand. But engineers starting from first-principles have no infrastructure to protect. They can question everything.

This is why breakthrough innovation almost never comes from industry leaders. It's not that they're stupid or lazy. It's that they're trapped in their assumption stack. Their expertise becomes their prison. As Upton Sinclair noted, "It is difficult to get a man to understand something when his salary depends on his not understanding it."

The Recursive Why: Engineering's Secret Weapon

Children drive parents crazy with endless "why" questions, but they're naturally doing what engineers must do deliberately: recursive interrogation of assumptions. Each "why" peels back a layer of convention to reveal underlying structure.

Musk describes this process explicitly: "When I interview someone to work at one of my companies, I ask them to tell me about the problems they worked on and how they solved them. And if someone was really the one who solved it, they'll be able to answer on multiple levels. They'll be able to go down to the brass tacks. And if they weren't, they'll get stuck."

The Recursive Why Applied to Rockets

"Why are rockets expensive?"

→ Because they're thrown away after one use.

"Why are they thrown away?"

→ Because they can't survive reentry.

"Why can't they survive reentry?"

→ They can, but they can't land precisely.

"Why can't they land precisely?"

→ They can, but it requires sophisticated guidance.

"Why don't they have sophisticated guidance?"

→ They do for going up. Nobody applied it to coming down.

"Why didn't anyone apply it?"

→ Because rockets were military missiles. Missiles don't need to land.

Each "why" revealed that the constraint wasn't physical but historical. Rockets were expensive because they inherited design assumptions from ICBMs, which were designed to deliver warheads, not return safely. The entire industry accepted single-use as inherent rather than inherited.

The recursive why works because each answer contains hidden assumptions. "They're thrown away after one use" assumes reuse is impossible. "They can't survive reentry" assumes current materials and designs. "It requires sophisticated guidance" assumes this is prohibitively complex. But when you reach physics (actual, fundamental physics), you find surprisingly few real constraints.

This is why engineers with physics backgrounds often create the most radical innovations. They're trained to trace everything back to first-principles. They know the difference between "this violates thermodynamics" (actually impossible) and "this violates industry practice" (merely difficult).

The Component Fallacy: Why Systems Thinking Matters

Here's where first-principles thinking gets subtle: you can't just decompose systems into components and rebuild. Systems have emergent properties that don't exist at the component level. This is the mistake many engineers make when they first attempt first-principles reasoning: they engage in reductionism without synthesis.

Consider Tesla's real innovation. It wasn't the battery (Panasonic made those). It wasn't the motor (AC induction motors existed). It wasn't even the software (though that was novel). Tesla's breakthrough was recognizing that an electric car isn't a car with an electric motor. It's a fundamentally different system.

Traditional Car vs. Tesla System Architecture

System Aspect	Traditional Car	Tesla
Drivetrain	Complex mechanical	Simple electric
Moving Parts	Hundreds	Dozen
Heat Management	Through radiation (waste)	Harvestable resource
Control Systems	Mechanical	Software
Service Model	Repairs as revenue	Updates as service
Infrastructure	Gasoline dependency	Electrical compatibility

The genius wasn't in the components but in recognizing that electric power enabled a completely different system architecture. Fewer parts meant higher reliability. Software control meant over-the-air updates. Battery placement meant better handling. Regenerative braking meant energy recovery. Each advantage cascaded through the system.

First principles thinking isn't just about decomposition. It's about recomposition with different organizing principles. You don't just break things down to physics and rebuild the same structure. You ask: given these physical possibilities, what's the optimal system architecture?

The Adjacent Possible: What Becomes Available Now

Stuart Kauffman's concept of the "adjacent possible" explains why first-principles thinking works better at some moments than others. The adjacent possible represents all the things that could be invented using currently available components and knowledge: one step away from current reality.

In 2003, Musk could attempt reusable rockets because several technologies had just entered the adjacent possible:

Technology	Why It Enabled Reusable Rockets (2003)
GPS	Precise enough for autonomous landing
Computational power	Real-time trajectory adjustment
Materials science	Light and strong enough for multiple launches
Sensors	Cheap enough for redundant systems
Software	Sophisticated enough for autonomous control

Twenty years earlier, these components weren't adjacent: they were multiple steps away. Twenty years later, they'd be a commodity. The window for radical innovation using these components was narrow.

First Principles Opportunity Scanner

Step	Question	Action
1. Identify Assumptions	What assumptions does your industry make?	Separate technical from business model assumptions
2. Test Against Physics	Which constraints are actually physics?	Keep real physical limits, question conventions
3. Test Against Regulations	Which constraints are regulations vs. tradition?	Navigate legal requirements, disrupt habits
4. Check Adjacent Possible	What's now possible that wasn't before?	Identify newly available technologies
5. Assess Market Readiness	What markets will accept radical change?	Find early adopters willing to experiment
6. Evaluate Improvement	Is 10x improvement possible?	If YES → Build from first-principles; If NO → Wait or find different problem

The adjacent possible also explains why some innovations fail despite being technically correct. Google Glass applied first-principles thinking to wearable computing, but the social infrastructure wasn't adjacent. The technology worked; society wasn't ready. Understanding the adjacent possible means knowing not just what physics allows but what the current moment enables.

The False Optimization Trap

The most dangerous assumption is optimization within constraints that shouldn't exist. Industries spend decades perfecting solutions to problems that first-principles thinking reveals aren't problems at all.

Consider home heating before heat pumps. The industry assumption stack:

1. Heating requires burning fuel or resistive electricity
2. Efficiency means better combustion or insulation
3. The goal is to generate heat

Generations of engineers optimized furnaces to 98% efficiency. But heat pumps revealed the entire framework was wrong. The goal isn't generating heat. It's moving heat. And moving heat can be 300-400% "efficient" because you're not creating energy, just relocating it. **The industry spent a century optimizing the wrong thing.**

Expertise in optimization can blind you to transformation. The better you get at solving the wrong problem, the harder it becomes to see that it's the wrong problem. This is why industries get disrupted by outsiders: insiders are too good at optimizing within false constraints.

The False Optimization Pattern

Industry	What They Optimized	What Disrupted Them
Film Photography	Perfected chemical processing	Digital eliminated chemistry
Typewriters	Perfected mechanical linkages	Word processors eliminated mechanics
Taxis	Optimized dispatch	Uber eliminated dispatch entirely
Hotels	Perfected hospitality	Airbnb eliminated hospitality model

This is why first-principles thinking is so powerful: it prevents you from becoming an expert at solving the wrong problem. Instead of asking "How can we make this better?" you ask "Should this exist at all?"

The Implementation Challenge: From Physics to Product

Here's the hard truth about first-principles thinking: being right about physics isn't enough. You still have to engineer a solution, build a company, and convince markets. This is where many engineers fail: they nail the physics but fumble the implementation.

Dyson was right about cyclonic separation in 1978. It took him until 1983 to build a working prototype and until 1993 to achieve market success. That's 15 years from first-principles insight to commercial victory. During those years, he was rejected by every major manufacturer, sued for patent infringement, and nearly went bankrupt multiple times.

The implementation challenge has three components:

Technical Implementation: Making physics work reliably at scale. SpaceX's first three rockets exploded. Tesla's first Roadsters had massive quality issues. First principles tell you something is possible; engineering makes it work.

Economic Implementation: Making physics work profitably. Concorde proved that supersonic passenger flight was physically possible but economically unviable with 1960s technology. First principles must eventually yield sustainable economics.

Social Implementation: Making physics work culturally. Segway applied first-principles to personal transportation but failed the social test. People felt ridiculous riding them. First principles can't ignore human psychology.

This is why successful first-principles innovators combine engineering insight with implementation persistence. They're not just right about physics. They're stubborn enough to spend years or decades making physics practical.

The Engineer's Edge

First principles thinking is the engineer's asymmetric advantage in innovation. While MBAs analyze markets and designers empathize with users, engineers can see through accumulated assumptions to fundamental reality. This isn't arrogance. It's a different lens for viewing problems.

But here's what's crucial: first-principles thinking isn't about being smarter. It's about being willing to look stupid. When Musk said he'd land rockets on boats, the aerospace industry laughed. When Stegra said they'd make steel without coal (questioning a 150-year-old industrial process), established steelmakers dismissed them as naive. When Tesla said cars could be computers, Detroit dismissed them as toys.

Looking stupid is the price of first-principles thinking. You're questioning assumptions that experts consider settled. You're proposing solutions that violate conventional wisdom. You're building things that shouldn't work according to industry knowledge. Of course, you look stupid until you succeed.

What I find liberating: engineers don't need permission to engage in first-principles thinking. You don't need market validation to question whether rockets must be expendable. You don't need customer interviews to explore hydrogen-based steel reduction. You don't need focus groups to investigate battery chemistry. You need physics knowledge, engineering skill, and the courage to ignore everyone who says it's impossible.

The engineer's advantage isn't just technical knowledge. It's the ability to distinguish between human rules and natural laws. Markets are human rules. Business models are human rules. Industry practices are human rules. Only physics is non-negotiable.

Everything else is up for renegotiation.

References

1. Clear, J. (2018). "First Principles: Elon Musk on the Power of Thinking for Yourself." JamesClear.com.
2. ASML. (2023). "Leading the Future of Lithography." Annual Report.
3. Vancc, A. (2015). Elon Musk: Tcsla, SpaceX, and the Quest for a Fantastic Future. Ecco.
4. Dyson, J. (1997). Against the Odds: An Autobiography. Orion Business.
5. Kauffman, S. (2000). Investigations. Oxford University Press.

CHAPTER 5

SYSTEMS THINKING VS. DESIGN THINKING

First principles reveal what physics allows. But building real systems requires understanding how components interact, which brings us to systems thinking. Design thinking and systems thinking approach the same problems from fundamentally different directions. Consider hospital emergency room wait times.

A design thinking approach interviews patients, creates journey maps, identifies pain points, and prototypes a better waiting experience: comfortable chairs, clear signage, and real-time updates. It makes waiting more pleasant. It doesn't question why the waiting exists.

A systems thinking approach maps patient flows, identifies bottlenecks, analyzes triage algorithms, and redesigns the entire emergency care system. It aims to eliminate waiting by restructuring how emergency medicine works.

Same problem, fundamentally different worldviews.

Design thinking asks, "What do users need?" Systems thinking asks, "What becomes possible?" Design thinking optimizes human experience within existing systems. Systems thinking questions whether those systems should exist. This isn't just a methodological difference; it's an epistemological chasm that explains why designers create better products while engineers create new realities.

Design thinking excels at refining meaning once capability exists. It struggles when the capability itself is unknown. The issue is not whether design thinking works, it's when it applies.

The Toyota Production System: When the System IS the Innovation

Before Taiichi Ohno revolutionized manufacturing at Toyota in the 1950s, the entire automotive industry operated on the same assumption: efficiency meant large batches. Ford's River Rouge plant epitomized this thinking: massive runs of identical parts, warehouses full of inventory, efficiency through scale.

Ohno asked a different question: What if inventory is waste, not efficiency? This wasn't improving the existing system; it was inverting its fundamental logic. As Ohno explained in his book, "All we are doing is looking at the timeline from the moment the customer gives us an order to the point when we collect the cash. And we are reducing that timeline by removing the non-value-added wastes."

Element	Description	Counterintuitive Aspect
Just-In-Time	Make only what's needed, when needed	Smaller batches eliminate waste
Kanban Cards	Visual signals trigger production	System self-regulates without planning
Continuous Flow	Single-piece flow, not batch	Car moves continuously, never waits
Jidoka	Machines stop on problems	Stops seem inefficient but prevent defects

Toyota didn't develop TPS through customer research. Customers weren't asking for lean manufacturing or just-in-time delivery. Ohno was thinking in systems: how do all the parts interact? What happens when you remove buffers? How does information flow trigger material flow?

By 1990, when Womack, Jones, and Roos published "The Machine That Changed the World," Toyota was producing cars with half the human effort, half the manufacturing space, half the engineering hours, and half the time to develop new products. They had fewer defects, smaller inventories, and greater variety. **The system itself was the innovation.**

However, blindly adopting these methods creates a dangerous trap. Before the COVID-19 pandemic, Just-In-Time (JIT) had devolved from a manufacturing insight into an ideology, a dogma taught in Six Sigma workshops and Lean Management seminars as the only way to operate. The focus shifted from understanding the system to blindly removing "waste."

When the pandemic hit, the fragility of this ideology was exposed. Global logistics collapsed because there were no buffers. Then, the market violently swung the other way: companies panicked and shifted from "Just-In-Time" to "Just-In-Case," hoarding materials and filling warehouses. This reactionary wave created even longer-lasting interruptions and component shortages than the initial disruption itself.

The economic irony is painful. The savings generated by JIT over 15–20 years had already been distributed to shareholders or reinvested; the money was gone. But the damage from the collapse happened all at once. Even if the long-term savings theoretically equaled the sudden cost of the crisis, the timing was asymmetric. A slow trickle of savings cannot offset a sudden, catastrophic bill.

True systems thinking isn't about following the wave of "Lean" or the counter-wave of "Hoarding." It is about asking: Does this specific system need efficiency, or does it need the redundancy to survive a crash? Ohno removed buffers to expose problems. If you remove buffers just to satisfy a dogma, without the capacity to survive the inevitable shock, you don't have a lean system; you have a broken one.

The ARPANET Lesson: Systems Before Users

In 1969, when the first ARPANET message traveled between UCLA and Stanford, nobody was thinking about user experience. The system crashed after transmitting "LO" of "LOGIN," but that wasn't seen as a failure. It was data about system behavior. This attitude would seem strange to modern designers, yet ARPANET became the internet, the most transformative technology of our era.

ARPANET's creators weren't trying to solve user problems. They were exploring what became possible when computers could communicate. J.C.R. Licklider's vision of "Intergalactic Computer Network" wasn't based on user research. It was based on understanding what distributed computing could enable.

The system design principles that emerged reveal systems thinking in its purest form:

End-to-End Principle: Intelligence at edges, simplicity in the middle. Users must handle complexity, not the network. This enables innovation at the edges without permission from the center.

Packet Switching: Data is broken into packets that find their own routes. Inefficient for any single transmission, but resilient for the system. No user asked for this; it emerged from systems analysis.

Protocol Layers: Separation of concerns across OSI layers. Incomprehensible to users, but it allowed independent evolution of each layer. HTTP could have been invented without rewiring routers.

No Central Control: Nobody owns the internet. This creates challenges users face (spam, security issues) but enables innovations users love (the web, streaming, social media).

Every attempt to make the internet more "user-friendly" through central control (AOL's walled garden, France's Minitel, various "information superhighway" proposals) failed. The messy, complex, systems-first approach won because it enabled possibilities that user-centered design would have prevented.

The Boeing 747 Gamble: Betting the Company on System Design

In 1965, Boeing faced a choice that would define aviation's future. Airlines wanted bigger planes, but they were thinking incrementally: stretch the 707, add more seats. Juan Trippe of Pan Am was thinking in systems: "I want a plane twice the size of anything flying." Not 20% bigger. Not 50% bigger. Double.

Boeing's board thought CEO Bill Allen had lost his mind when he committed to building the 747. The development cost ($2 billion) exceeded Boeing's entire value. But Allen wasn't thinking about planes; he was thinking about systems. What happens to aviation when you can move 400 people at once?

The 747's design reveals systems thinking at every level:

The Distinctive Hump: Not an aesthetic choice but a systems solution. Cargo variants needed a front-loading door. Put the cockpit above the cargo deck. The hump that resulted became the 747's signature, but it was systems logic, not styling.

Wide-Body Configuration: Two aisles instead of one. This wasn't primarily about passenger comfort. It was about boarding/

deplaning logistics. Halving the time at gates meant doubling aircraft utilization.

High-Bypass Turbofan Engines: Quieter, more efficient, but massive. Required completely new engine pylons, wing structures, and maintenance procedures. The entire aviation ecosystem had to evolve.

Modular Interior: Seats, galleys, and lavatories could be reconfigured overnight. Airlines initially resisted (they wanted custom interiors). Boeing insisted on modularity. This system decision enabled the 747 to serve every market from budget charter to luxury first class.

Boeing didn't ask passengers what they wanted. Passengers would have said "more legroom" or "better food." Boeing asked what happened to the aviation system when transcontinental flight became economical for ordinary people. The answer reshaped global culture: suddenly, international travel was democratized.

Unix Philosophy: The Power of Compositional Systems

In 1969, Ken Thompson at Bell Labs started writing Unix because he wanted to play a game called Space Travel on a PDP-7 computer. This inauspicious beginning led to an operating system philosophy that would influence all subsequent software development. The Unix philosophy represents systems thinking in its purest form.

Doug McIlroy articulated it best: "Write programs that do one thing and do it well. Write programs to work together. Write programs to handle text streams, because that is a universal interface."

This approach created something remarkable:

Small, Composable Tools: Instead of monolithic applications, Unix provided tiny utilities (ls, grep, awk, sed) that could be combined in infinite ways. Users had to learn composition, but gained unlimited power.

Everything is a File: Devices, processes, network connections: all treated as files. This abstraction enables elegant system design.

Pipes and Redirection: The ability to chain programs together (ls | grep | sort | uniq) requires users to think in terms of data streams and transformation rather than applications. Harder to learn, infinitely more powerful.

Unix principles underlie Android, iOS, macOS, and virtually every server on the internet. Why? Systems thinking creates generative platforms, while product thinking creates consumable applications. Unix's compositional philosophy enabled innovations its creators never imagined. Every time someone writes a shell script that combines 20-year-old utilities in a new way, they're innovating without permission.

The Two Questions That Define Everything

Design Thinking Asks	Systems Thinking Asks	Result
What do users need?	What becomes possible?	Better version vs New capability
How might we solve?	What are the constraints?	Solution vs Architecture
Is this desirable?	How do parts interact?	Product vs System
Will people pay?	What emerges at scale?	Market fit vs Emergence

These questions lead to radically different innovations:

Design Approach: Uber made taxi-hailing better. The user's need was clear: "I want a taxi now." The solution was elegant: push a button, get a ride.

Systems Approach: Bitcoin created programmable money. No user asked for this. Satoshi Nakamoto asked: "What becomes possible with distributed consensus?" The answer enabled not just cryptocurrency but smart contracts, DeFi, NFTs: an entire parallel financial system.

Design thinking works backward from user needs to solutions. Systems thinking works forward from capabilities to applications.

The Feedback Loop Problem

Systems have a characteristic that makes them fundamentally different from products: feedback loops. Change one element, and effects cascade through the system, often in unexpected ways.

Consider Facebook's evolution:

Initial State: Students want to connect with classmates. Solution: College network.

First-Order Effect: Students connect. Success!

Second-Order Effects: Information cascades, social comparison, FOMO, political polarization, mental health impacts, and democracy effects.

No amount of user research in 2004 would have predicted teenage depression rates correlating with Instagram usage. Users couldn't articulate fears about algorithmic radicalization because the concept didn't exist. Systems thinking would have asked: "What happens when billions of people's social interactions are mediated by engagement algorithms?"

This is why systems thinking is essential for breakthrough innovation: it considers emergence, feedback loops, and unintended consequences.

The Systems Thinking Canvas

Based on these insights, I've developed a Systems Thinking Canvas that starts from capabilities, not customers:

Dimension	Question	Internet Example
Core Capability	What new thing can we do?	Computers can communicate
Constraint Removal	What limitation disappears?	Geographic distance for information
System Components	What are the essential parts?	Protocols, routers, endpoints
Interaction Rules	How do parts communicate?	TCP/IP, HTTP, DNS
Emergent Properties	What arises from interactions?	Web, email, social media
Feedback Loops	What reinforces or dampens?	Network effects, Metcalfe's Law
Scale Effects	What changes at 10x, 100x, 1000x?	Personal → Social → Cultural transformation
System Boundaries	What's inside vs. outside?	Edge devices vs. core infrastructure
Evolution Path	How might the system grow?	Static pages → Dynamic → Interactive → AI

This canvas doesn't start with users because users aren't the starting point for systems innovation. The point is understanding what the system enables. Users come later, usually using the system in ways you never imagined.

Why Engineers Default to Systems Thinking

Engineers think in systems because physical reality operates in systems. You can't wish your way around thermodynamics. You can't negotiate with electrons. Physical systems have non-negotiable rules that must be understood.

This creates a different mental model:

Design Thinkers see the world as problems to solve for people. Pain points to address. Experiences to improve. Stories to tell.

Systems Thinkers see the world as interconnected components with emergent behaviors. Constraints to navigate. Feedback loops to manage. Possibilities to explore.

When an engineer looks at traffic, they don't just see frustrated drivers: they see flow dynamics, bottlenecks, and queuing theory. The solution isn't necessarily making waiting more pleasant; it might be eliminating the systemic causes of waiting.

The most successful tech companies were founded by systems thinkers:

- **Google:** PageRank was a system's insight into link structure
- **Amazon:** "Everything Store" was systems thinking about logistics and inventory
- **Netflix:** Streaming was a systems bet on bandwidth trends
- **Tesla:** Electric vehicles as computers were systems architecture

These companies later hired designers to polish the user experience, but the breakthrough innovations came from systems thinking.

The Synthesis Challenge

Here's where things get nuanced: pure systems thinking creates powerful but inaccessible technologies. Pure design thinking creates pleasant but limited experiences. The challenge is synthesis.

Consider the iPhone's development. The breakthrough was systems thinking: Steve Jobs realized that miniaturized components (CPU, memory, battery, touchscreen) had reached a threshold where a pocket computer was possible. This wasn't user research; it was understanding the adjacent possible in component systems.

But then came the interface design. Making this pocket computer feel magical rather than complex. The genius was hiding the system complexity (Unix underneath, file system invisible) while exposing its capabilities (multitouch, apps, sensors).

The important realization: systems thinking came first. Design polished what systems thinking made possible. You can't design your way to breakthrough innovation, but you need design to make systems innovation accessible.

The optimal approach:

1. Systems thinking to identify what's possible
2. Build a proof of concept, ignoring user experience
3. Validate that the system works
4. Layer design to make it accessible
5. Iterate between system capabilities and user experience

This is different from starting with users. Users can't want what they can't imagine. Systems thinking reveals what's possible. Design makes it desirable. But possibility must come first.

User Experience: Essential, Not First

A critical clarification: This isn't an argument against user-centered design or user experience. Both are absolutely essential for breakthrough innovations to succeed. The question is when they matter most.

The optimal sequence for breakthrough innovation places technical validation before experience optimization:

Systems Thinking → Technical Breakthrough: Build the capability that didn't exist before. Prove the physics works. You're solving "Can this exist?", not yet "Will people use this?"

Proof of Concept → Complete Product: Progress through technical validation until the innovation is complete enough to evaluate with real users.

User Experience → Accessibility: Now apply user-centered design. Make the breakthrough accessible, delightful, and intuitive. This is where designers become critical partners, not because UX wasn't important before, but because premature UX optimization wastes effort on features that might not survive technical validation.

Market Feedback → Refinement: Customer development becomes powerful when users react to real capability, not imaginary futures.

Consider the iPhone: Apple spent years solving multi-touch sensing, mobile GPU acceleration, battery life, and miniaturization before applying legendary design polish. The rounded corners and slide-to-unlock came after the fundamental capability existed. Starting with user research would have yielded requests for better BlackBerry keyboards, not multi-touch screens that didn't yet exist.

Similarly, Tesla's Roadster proved that electric vehicles could be desirable despite mediocre UX. Model S added design refinement.

Model 3 achieved mass-market polish. The sequence: prove capability → refine design → scale with excellence.

Note for Designers and Engineers: This isn't UX-never, it's UX-when. Build breakthrough capability first, then make it accessible through excellent UX. Don't confuse the sequence with relative importance. User experience is how breakthrough innovations reach their potential, but you need the breakthrough before you can experience it. You can't design experiences around capabilities that don't yet exist.

The Power of Systems Perspective

The liberating insight for engineers: you don't need to apologize for thinking in systems rather than stories. The ability to see interconnections, feedback loops, and emergent properties isn't a deficiency. It's a superpower for innovation. The world has plenty of people making existing systems more user-friendly. It needs more people questioning whether those systems should exist at all.

Design thinking optimizes experiences. Systems thinking creates realities.

But systems thinking alone isn't enough. You also need time to build those systems properly: time for your technical approach to compound into something competitors cannot easily replicate. This raises the question the startup world obsesses over: Does being first to market matter? Or does building the best system matter more?

References

1. Ohno, T. (1988). Toyota Production System: Beyond Large-Scale Production. Productivity Press.
2. Womack, J. P., Jones, D. T., & Roos, D. (1990). The Machine That Changed the World: The Story of Lean Production. Free Press.
3. Abbate, J. (1999). Inventing the Internet. MIT Press.
4. Raymond, E. S. (2003). The Art of Unix Programming. Addison-Wesley.
5. Isaacson, W. (2011). Steve Jobs. Simon & Schuster.

CHAPTER 6

TECHNICAL MOATS

I n 1998, Google entered the search market with seventeen established competitors. AltaVista had a 50% market share. Yahoo was the internet's front door. Excite, Lycos, and Ask Jeeves had millions of users and hundreds of millions in funding. By every rule of startup timing, Google was catastrophically late. They should have failed.

They didn't. And their victory reveals why technical excellence creates more durable competitive advantages than being first to market. The startup world obsesses over timing: catching the wave, finding product-market fit before competitors, the mythical first-mover advantage. But history shows that the best technology usually wins, even if it arrives last. This is the engineer's ultimate vindication: building something genuinely better matters more than building something first.

Google's Late Arrival: How PageRank Ate the Internet

To understand Google's impossible victory, we need to examine what search looked like in 1998. AltaVista indexed 150 million pages, massive for the time. Their engineers had solved hard problems: crawling the nascent web, indexing at scale, and returning results quickly. They'd won. The market had spoken.

But AltaVista had optimized for the wrong metric. They measured success by index size and query speed. Their searches returned pages that contained your keywords, technically correct but practically useless. Searching for "Stanford University" might return a random student's page that mentions Stanford a dozen times before returning Stanford's actual homepage.

Larry Page and Sergey Brin asked a different question: not "Which pages contain these words?" but "Which pages do other pages think are authoritative?" PageRank wasn't just a better algorithm. It was a different conception of what search meant.

Google didn't need to be first because they'd found a technical insight that made existing approaches obsolete. PageRank treated the web as a graph, not a collection of documents. Links were votes. Important pages had more votes. Pages voted on by important pages mattered more. This recursive definition created a technical moat that competitors couldn't cross.

The Three Layers of Google's Moat

Layer	What It Required	Why Competitors Couldn't Cross
Mathematical Foundation	Linear algebra eigenvector calculations	Fundamentally different math
Computational Requirement	Processing entire web graph repeatedly	Requires massive infrastructure
Feedback Loop	More users → better data → better algorithm	Technical advantage compounds

AltaVista tried to copy PageRank once they understood it, but they faced an impossible choice: abandon their existing technology (and advantage) to chase Google, or try to bolt PageRank onto their keyword-based system. They chose the compromise and got the worst of both worlds.

Being late helped Google. They could see what everyone else had tried. They knew keyword-based search hit fundamental limits. They knew portals (Yahoo's strategy) created editorial bottlenecks. They knew human-curated directories (Ask Jeeves) couldn't scale. By arriving last, they could build the right thing instead of the first thing.

TSMC's Manufacturing Moat: The Power of Pure Play

Taiwan Semiconductor Manufacturing Company (TSMC) represents perhaps the deepest technical moat in modern technology. Founded in 1987, TSMC didn't invent semiconductors: they were decades late to that party. Intel, Texas Instruments, and Fairchild had defined the industry. But TSMC's founder, Morris Chang, saw something others missed: chip design and chip manufacturing were different competencies that didn't need to live in the same company.

This "pure play" foundry model seemed absurd. Why would chip designers trust their most valuable intellectual property to an external manufacturer? Why would a manufacturer invest billions without designing their own chips? The industry laughed. Intel's Andy Grove famously dismissed the foundry model as fundamentally flawed.

But TSMC's technical moat grew deeper every year:

Process Excellence: By focusing solely on manufacturing, TSMC could invest more in process technology than integrated manufacturers. They didn't dilute R&D across design and manufacturing. Every dollar went toward making chips better, smaller, faster.

Customer Learning: Each customer taught TSMC something new. Apple pushed them on power efficiency. Nvidia on performance. Qualcomm on integration. This diverse learning accelerated their technical development in ways Intel's internal focus couldn't match.

Scale Economics: As more designers chose TSMC, they could afford more advanced equipment. More advanced equipment attracted more designers. The cycle compounded. By 2023, TSMC commanded more than 50% of the global foundry market share and over 90% of advanced node production.

EUV Lithography Mastery: When extreme ultraviolet (EUV) lithography emerged as essential for sub-7nm chips, TSMC partnered with ASML (the only EUV equipment maker) to master this impossibly complex technology. As Chris Miller documents in "Chip War," each EUV machine costs $200 million, requires multiple 747s to transport, and uses lasers that vaporize tin droplets 50,000 times per second to generate light. TSMC owns more EUV machines than anyone else and has the deepest expertise in using them.

But ASML's monopoly depends on an even deeper moat: Carl Zeiss SMT's optics. The German company, drawing on 175+ years of optical expertise, holds a 100% monopoly on EUV optical systems. No other company on Earth can manufacture the mirrors precisely enough for EUV wavelengths, each mirror polished to atomic smoothness, with surface irregularities measured in picometers. TRUMPF, another German family-owned company (100% privately held since 1923), supplies the ultra-high-power CO_2 lasers that generate the EUV light. This German-Dutch supply chain represents perhaps the deepest technical moat in modern manufacturing: three companies whose combined expertise took decades to accumulate and cannot be bypassed.

TSMC's moat isn't just about having expensive equipment. It's about accumulated learning from running that equipment 24/7 for years. Intel can buy the same ASML machines, but it can't buy TSMC's decade of experience pushing those machines to their limits.

ARM's Licensing Revolution: Why Architecture Beats Implementation

ARM Holdings represents perhaps the purest example of technical moats defeating market timing. In 1990, when ARM spun out of Acorn Computers, Intel had already won the processor wars. x86 dominated PCs. RISC had lost. The market was over.

But ARM did something nobody expected: they stopped making chips. Instead, they licensed chip designs. This wasn't pivoting. It was recognizing that their technical advantage wasn't in manufacturing but in architecture.

The ARM architecture had been designed for the Acorn Archimedes computer with brutal constraints: minimal power consumption, a simple instruction set, and efficient execution. These constraints, which seemed like weaknesses in the PC era, became superpowers in the mobile era.

ARM created a technical moat through architectural elegance, not manufacturing prowess:

Fundamentally Efficient: RISC (Reduced Instruction Set Computing) meant fewer transistors, less power, and less heat. While Intel added features, ARM removed them.

Infinitely Customizable: Licensees could modify ARM designs for specific needs. Apple could optimize for phones, Qualcomm for modems, and Nvidia for graphics. Intel's one-size-fits-all approach couldn't compete.

Ecosystem-Enabling: By licensing rather than manufacturing, ARM created an ecosystem where hundreds of companies could innovate on ARM architecture. Each innovation strengthened ARM's moat.

The technical moat was so strong that Intel, with unlimited resources and decades of experience, couldn't cross it. They spent billions trying to compete in mobile with x86. They failed so completely that they exited the mobile chip business entirely.

By 2020, ARM processors were in 95% of smartphones, 90% of tablets, and increasingly in laptops and servers. Apple's M1 chip, based on ARM architecture, outperformed Intel's best processors while using a fraction of the power. The company that was "too late" to the processor market ended up defining mobile computing.

BYD's Battery Integration: From Phones to Cars

BYD (Build Your Dreams) started in 1995, making batteries for mobile phones, hardly a cutting-edge technology. The lithium-ion battery market was dominated by Japanese giants like Sony and Panasonic. By traditional market timing logic, BYD was hopelessly late. But founder Wang Chuanfu, a chemist, saw technical opportunities others missed.

Manufacturing Innovation: While competitors focused on battery chemistry, BYD revolutionized manufacturing. They replaced expensive automated Japanese production lines with semi-automated processes using cheap Chinese labor. This wasn't just cost-cutting. It allowed rapid iteration and customization that fully automated lines couldn't match.

Vertical Integration: BYD made everything in-house: from lithium processing to battery management systems. When they entered electric vehicles, they made the batteries, motors, semiconductors, and even the plastic interiors. This integration created compound technical advantages that competitors couldn't replicate.

Blade Battery Breakthrough: In 2020, BYD introduced the Blade Battery. Lithium iron phosphate (LFP) cells are arranged in a blade-like formation that becomes a structural element of the car itself. This eliminated the need for modules and reduced weight while improving safety. The design was so elegant that Tesla licensed it for their standard-range vehicles.

Chemistry Expertise: While others chased energy density with nickel-rich chemistries, BYD perfected safer, cheaper LFP batteries. They overcame LFP's traditional weakness (low energy density) through cell-to-pack integration that eliminated wasted space.

By 2023, BYD had become the world's second-largest EV battery maker with 17% global market share, behind only CATL. More impressively, they'd become the world's largest EV manufacturer by volume, surpassing Tesla in Q4 2023. The company that started making phone batteries when that market was already mature had built an unassailable position in transportation electrification.

BYD demonstrates that technical moats can be built through integration and manufacturing excellence, not just breakthrough inventions.

Smartex: Industrial AI from Portugal

While Silicon Valley chases consumer AI applications, a Portuguese company has built a technical moat in an unglamorous but lucrative domain: textile defect detection. Smartex, founded in Porto, installs hardware directly inside knitting machines to detect flaws in real-time, stopping production before defective fabric is produced.

The technical moat has multiple layers:

Hardware-Software Integration: Smartex doesn't just sell software. Their system integrates cameras, lighting, and AI processing directly into manufacturing equipment. This isn't an app you download; it's physical infrastructure that becomes part of the production line.

Training Data Advantage: Every installation generates proprietary training data. Defects in cotton behave differently from defects in synthetics. Each factory's equipment has unique characteristics. Smartex's AI improves with every meter of fabric inspected, creating a compounding advantage competitors can't replicate without similar deployments.

Domain Expertise: Understanding textile manufacturing requires years of industry knowledge. The founders didn't just build AI; they learned how knitting machines work, how fabric defects form, and how factory economics function. This domain knowledge is as much a moat as the technology itself.

After winning the Web Summit PITCH in 2021, Smartex raised $24.7 million in Series A funding led by Lightspeed Venture Partners and Tony Fadell's Build Collective. They now operate globally with offices in Porto, San Francisco, and Shenzhen.

Smartex illustrates a pattern worth noting: the most durable technical moats often come from solving "boring" infrastructure problems rather than chasing consumer trends.

Qualcomm's Patent Fortress: Engineering Around the Impossible

Qualcomm's dominance in mobile communications reveals another form of technical moat: solving problems others consider impossible. In the 1980s, the telecommunications industry had settled on TDMA (Time Division Multiple Access) for digital cellular. The standards were set. The battles were over.

Irwin Jacobs and Andrew Viterbi disagreed. They believed CDMA (Code Division Multiple Access), a technology used by the military for secure communications, could work for cellular. The industry's response was unanimous: impossible. CDMA was too complex, too power-hungry, too expensive for consumer devices.

Here's what the experts "knew": CDMA required precise power control (impossible in mobile devices), complex signal processing (too expensive for handsets), and GPS-synchronized base stations (impractical for cellular networks). Each objection was technically correct given 1980s technology.

But Jacobs and Viterbi saw what others missed: Moore's Law would solve the complexity problem. DSP chips would get powerful enough. GPS would become ubiquitous. They weren't building for today's constraints but tomorrow's capabilities.

Qualcomm spent seven years and nearly went bankrupt multiple times, proving CDMA could work. When they finally demonstrated a working system in 1989, the industry's response shifted from "impossible" to "impractical." When they launched commercially in 1995, it shifted again to "unnecessary."

Then the data era arrived. CDMA's technical advantages (higher capacity, better spectrum efficiency, superior data rates) became essential. The technology everyone said was impossible became the foundation of 3G, 4G, and 5G networks.

The Technical Moat Assessment Framework

Based on these patterns, I've developed the Technical Moat Assessment framework for evaluating whether technical advantages will endure:

Depth Dimension: How Hard to Replicate?

Level	Advantage Type	Characteristics	Moat Duration
1	Feature Advantage (Shallow)	Better UI, performance optimization, feature completeness	6-12 months
2	Architectural Advantage (Moderate)	Superior system design, better algorithmic approach, elegant abstraction	2-3 years
3	Mathematical/ Physical Advantage (Deep)	Fundamental breakthrough, novel approach to physics, new mathematical framework	5-10 years
4	Compound Advantage (Deepest)	Multiple reinforcing advantages, network effects plus technical superiority, system that improves with scale	10+ years

Width Dimension: How Much to Replicate?

Width	Scope	Example
Narrow	Single component or algorithm	PageRank alone
Moderate	Multiple integrated systems	ARM architecture
Wide	Entire technology stack	Qualcomm's CDMA system
Ecosystem	Technology plus developer tools, partnerships, standards	TSMC's manufacturing ecosystem

Defensibility Factors

Technical Moat Score = Depth × Width × Defensibility

Defensibility includes: Patents (legal protection), Trade Secrets (hidden knowledge), Complexity (integration challenges), Data Advantage (learning from usage), Talent Concentration (key people), Capital Requirements (cost to replicate), Time Requirements (years to catch up).

The strongest position is deep, wide moats with multiple defensibility factors.

Why First-Mover Advantage Is Usually a Disadvantage

The startup world's obsession with first-mover advantage is particularly puzzling given the evidence:

Market	First Movers	Winner
Search	AltaVista, Excite, Lycos	Google (late entrant)
Social Networks	Friendster, MySpace	Facebook (late entrant)
Smartphones	BlackBerry, Palm	iPhone (late entrant)
Electric Vehicles	GM's EV1 (1996), Nissan Leaf (2010)	Tesla (late but better)
Cloud Computing	Loudcloud, Exodus	AWS (late entrant)
Semiconductors	Fairchild, Intel	TSMC (late pure-play) dominates advanced nodes

The pattern is consistent: first movers explore the space, make mistakes, educate the market, and then get replaced by late entrants with superior technology.

The Compound Interest of Technical Excellence

Here's what the business world doesn't understand about technical moats: they compound. Every technical advantage makes the next one easier to build. This is why technology companies exhibit winner-take-all dynamics that confuse traditional business analysis.

Consider Tesla's compounding technical advantages:

Battery Expertise → Better range and performance → More customer data → Better Autopilot training → More valuable car → Higher margins → More R&D investment → Better batteries

Each cycle strengthens every advantage. A competitor can't just match one aspect: they need to match the entire reinforcing system. By the time they catch up to where Tesla is today, Tesla has compounded several more cycles ahead.

Important caveat: Tesla's success with this approach is notable precisely because it's exceptional. Fisker Automotive, Better Place, and Coda Automotive all pursued similar EV strategies with significant capital and failed. The compounding advantage strategy works, but execution risk is enormous, and failure is far more common than success.

The crucial pattern: technical moats create time advantages that money can't overcome. You can't hire your way to ten years of production battery data. You can't acquire your way to a million cars collecting autopilot training data. You can't fundraise your way to years of manufacturing learning.

This is why technical founders often defeat business founders in technology markets. Business founders optimize for market timing, fundraising, and go-to-market. Technical founders optimize for building something competitors can't replicate. In the short term, business founders often win. In the long term, technical moats determine the winner.

The False God of Network Effects

The startup world worships network effects as the ultimate moat, but network effects without technical differentiation are surprisingly fragile:

Incumbent	Network Effects	Challenger	Technical Superiority	Outcome
SMS	Everyone had a phone number	WhatsApp	Internet-based, rich media, groups	Technical superiority won
Email	Everyone had an address	Slack	Channels, integrations, search	Technical superiority winning
Skype	Hundreds of millions of users	Zoom	It just worked	Technical superiority won

The pattern is clear: network effects create switching costs, but technical superiority creates switching benefits. When the benefit exceeds the cost, users switch despite network effects.

The strongest moats combine network effects with technical superiority. Google has network effects (more users → more data → better results) built on technical superiority (PageRank and its descendants). Facebook has network effects (your friends are there) built on technical superiority (infrastructure that serves billions efficiently).

Pure network effects are the business school's moat. Technical superiority is the engineering school's moat. When they compete, engineering usually wins, because network effects can be overcome, but physics can't.

The Patient Path to Technical Dominance

Technical moats require patience that the modern startup ecosystem doesn't encourage. You can't growth-hack your way to technical superiority. You can't blitzscale fundamental research. You can't pivot your way to breakthrough insights.

Building technical moats requires:

Deep Work: Years of focused research on hard problems. Google's founders spent two years on PageRank before starting the company. ARM spent a decade perfecting its architecture. Qualcomm nearly went bankrupt, proving CDMA worked. TSMC spent decades mastering manufacturing. BYD spent years perfecting battery integration.

Ignoring Market Feedback: The market will tell you to build something easier, faster, and more conventional. Tesla was told electric cars should be cheap commuters. Google was told that search was commoditized. ARM was told RISC was dead. TSMC was told that integrated manufacturing was superior.

Compound Patience: Technical advantages compound slowly, then suddenly. For years, you've looked like you're falling behind. Then your technical moat becomes unassailable, and you dominate for decades.

The liberating realization: engineers don't need to race to market. While MBAs are pivoting and growth-hacking, you can be building something genuinely better. While they're optimizing for investor metrics, you can be optimizing for technical excellence.

The deepest technical moats often look like bad ideas for years. Qualcomm's CDMA was "impossible." Google's PageRank was "academic." Tesla's electric vehicles were "toys." TSMC's pure-play model was "flawed." BYD's LFP batteries were "inferior." But patient technical excellence eventually defeats impatient market timing.

Build the moat. The timing takes care of itself.

Technical excellence creates moats. But how do you build excellence when resources are scarce? The conventional wisdom says you need venture capital, large teams, and unlimited funding. The evidence suggests otherwise.

References

1. Miller, C. (2022). Chip War: The Fight for the World's Most Critical Technology. Scribner.
2. TSMC. (2023). "Technology Leadership, Manufacturing Excellence, Customer Trust." Annual Report.
3. Brin, S., & Page, L. (1998). "The Anatomy of a Large-Scale Hypertextual Web Search Engine." Stanford University.
4. ARM Holdings. (1990–2020). Annual Reports.
5. BYD. (2020–2023). Annual Reports.

CHAPTER 7

THE BOOTSTRAP CHOICE

At startup conferences, you see a strange ritual: engineers apologizing for building profitable businesses. "We're still bootstrapping," they confess, as if this were a failure rather than a strategy. VCs nod sympathetically, offering to "help" with introductions. The unspoken message is clear: real companies raise capital.

When did building a business with customer money become something to apologize for?

Dr. Dileep Rao's research into billion-dollar entrepreneurs revealed a pattern that should reshape how we think about funding innovation. Studying every entrepreneur who built a billion-dollar company from scratch in America from 1946 onward, he found that 94% succeeded without early-stage venture capital. Within this group, 76% never used VC at all, while 18% delayed it until after proving their business model.

Important Context: This 94% figure reflects companies built primarily before 2000, when venture capital was less available and geographically concentrated. Today's innovation ecosystem has largely inverted: among current unicorns (1,200+ companies), approximately 95% are VC-funded, with a median funding of $275 million. (Note: These figures use different baselines. Rao studied companies that reached $1B valuation from scratch, while the current unicorn lists include companies at all funding stages.) However, this shift reflects ecosystem availability rather than validation that VC is necessary for breakthrough innovation. The outliers (Mailchimp's $12B bootstrapped exit, Epic Systems' $3.8B revenue without ever raising VC, Zoho's $1B+ revenue) prove the bootstrap path remains viable and often superior for patient, technical innovation when pursued strategically.

The crucial distinction: understanding when bootstrapping serves your innovation better than venture capital ever could.

The Tale of Two Eras

Rao's methodology was rigorous, interviewing 116 unicorn entrepreneurs and analyzing 125 companies that achieved both billion-dollar sales and valuations. His findings reflected companies like Microsoft, Dell, Bloomberg, and Walmart, enterprises that bootstrapped or self-funded their way to dominance in an era before the current VC explosion.

The distinction matters profoundly. Pre-2000 entrepreneurs faced different constraints: venture capital was geographically concentrated in Silicon Valley and Boston, focused primarily on hardware and telecommunications, and represented a fraction of today's $170+ billion annual deployment. Building software required millions in upfront infrastructure costs. Distribution meant physical media or expensive enterprise sales teams. The bootstrap path wasn't just viable. It was often the only path.

Today's landscape presents a paradox. Venture capital has never been more available, yet the fundamental economics that made bootstrapping superior haven't changed. The 94% who succeeded without early VC fell into patterns that remain instructive: some bootstrapped to profitability entirely, funding growth through customers rather than investors; others used revenue-funded growth, letting early sales finance expansion at sustainable rates;

many leveraged strategic angels who provided expertise without demanding the 100x returns that distort company development. In Deep Tech, particularly, SBIR/STTR grants and government contracts provided patient capital without equity dilution.

The contemporary bootstrap successes follow these same patterns, just at an accelerated scale.

The Modern Bootstrap Titans

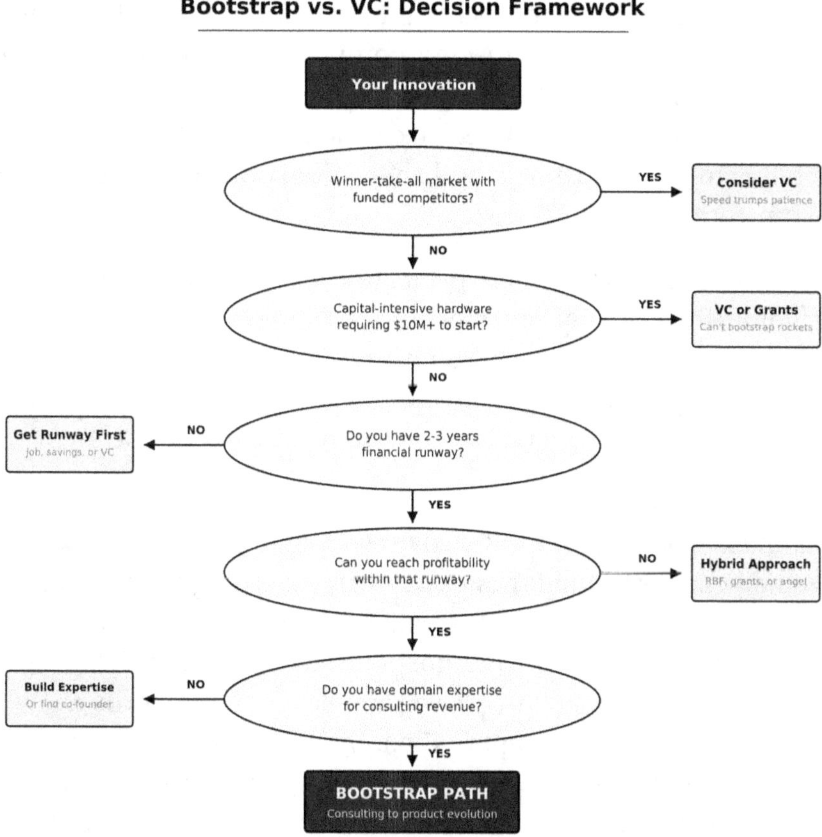

Consider Mailchimp's trajectory. Ben Chestnut and Dan Kurzius started in 2001 as a web design agency, building email tools for clients as a side project. No grand vision. No pitch decks.

Just solving their own problem. For eight years, they ran Mailchimp as a lifestyle business, content with modest profits and sustainable growth.

The pivotal moment came in 2009 when they introduced a freemium model, not because VCs demanded growth, but because they could afford to experiment. With no investors to satisfy, they could take the long-term risk of giving away their product. Revenue exploded from $5 million to $700 million over the next decade, all without external funding.

In 2021, Intuit acquired Mailchimp for $12 billion: the largest acquisition of a bootstrapped company in history. Chestnut and Kurzius owned 100% of the company. As Chestnut told the Financial Times: "I kind of feel like I had my head down, tweaking things, improving things, and then I looked up and bam, it's a $12bn company."

Epic Systems represents an even purer example of patient capital triumph. In 1979, Judy Faulkner started the company with $70,000: half from her own savings, half from friends and family. Her goal wasn't to flip a startup but to build software that actually worked for healthcare providers. No VCs. No pivots. No exit strategy.

Epic chose the hardest possible market (healthcare) and the most complex product (comprehensive electronic health records). VCs would have demanded they start with something simpler, iterate faster, and show traction. Instead, Faulkner spent years building deep, complex systems that hospitals could trust with life-and-death decisions. By 2023, Epic will handle medical records for over 250 million Americans, approximately 75% of the US population. Annual revenue exceeds $3.8 billion. The company remains 100% employee-owned, with Faulkner worth over $7 billion, having never diluted a single share.

Zoho offers a global perspective on bootstrapping. Founded in 1996 by Sridhar Vembu and Tony Thomas in Chennai, India, the company has grown to over $1 billion in revenue with 15,000 employees across 10 countries. Vembu's philosophy explicitly rejects Silicon Valley orthodoxy. "I don't like the word exit," he has said, viewing the concept as antithetical to building something lasting. He stays out of the VC ecosystem because, as he puts it, "a lot of venture capital is driven around exits" rather than long-term company building.

Why Engineers Hold the Bootstrap Advantage

Engineers possess unique advantages for bootstrapping that business-focused founders lack. The most fundamental is technical leverage: you can build the product yourself. While non-technical founders need to hire developers at $150- 150- 200k salaries, burning through capital before writing a line of code, you can create the entire technical foundation solo or with a small team. This changes the economics fundamentally.

Research from the European Innovation Council shows that technical founders achieve 2.3x higher capital efficiency than non-technical founders in early stages. The reasons compound: a laptop, cloud credits, and determination can take you surprisingly far. You don't need offices to impress investors, PR agencies to generate buzz, or business development teams to hustle partnerships. The engineer's natural habitat (a quiet room with a good computer) is also the ideal bootstrapping environment.

The product-first culture that gets engineers criticized in VC circles becomes a strength when bootstrapping. You're not burning money on premature scaling or customer acquisition before the product works. German Mittelstand companies exemplify this approach: family-owned engineering firms that dominate global niches through technical excellence rather than marketing spend. As Hermann Simon documented in "Hidden Champions," these companies average 70% global market share in their niches while remaining largely unknown to the general public.

Perhaps most powerfully, the engineering community's culture of open-source means you can build on enormous foundations of free, high-quality code. Your innovation can focus on the differentiator, not rebuilding the basics. JetBrains proved that engineers will happily pay for technical excellence. Starting in 2000, three programmers built development tools in Prague with no outside funding, competing against free alternatives from Microsoft and Google. The company generates hundreds of millions in annual revenue while remaining private and founder-controlled.

Engineers don't need VC funding because they can directly create value. MBAs need funding to hire people who create value. This isn't a subtle difference. It's a fundamental restructuring of startup economics.

The Hidden Costs of Venture Capital

The current reality that 95% of unicorns are VC-funded obscures a crucial question: at what cost? The transformation that occurs when a company takes early-stage venture capital goes far beyond equity dilution.

"In a world where companies are valued on growth metrics rather than profitability, the pressure to grow at all costs can destroy what made a company special in the first place." — Peter Thiel.

This control manifests most destructively in the growth mandate. VCs need 10x returns to make their portfolio math work, forcing unsustainable growth rates and often company destruction in pursuit of unicorn outcomes. The time horizon mismatch becomes fatal: VC funds have 7-10 year lifecycles, so your 20-year vision becomes their 5-year sprint.

The VC Transformation Machine

Your Company Goes In	Your Company Comes Out
Technical Excellence	Growth Metrics
Product Focus	Sales Focus
Engineering Culture	Growth Hacker Culture
Sustainable Pace	Burnout Pace
Your Vision	Pattern-Matched Vision
20-Year Horizon	5-Year Exit
100% Ownership	10-15% Ownership

Research from MIT Sloan reveals that VC-backed companies are 2.7x more likely to shut down entirely rather than achieve sustainable profitability compared to bootstrapped competitors. The pressure for hypergrowth creates what Ross and Fonstad call "premature scaling syndrome": companies optimizing for metrics that attract the next funding round rather than building lasting value.

The Profitability Postponement Paradox

Perhaps nothing illustrates the VC distortion more clearly than the current AI gold rush. Companies with billion-dollar valuations and zero path to profitability are celebrated as successes. OpenAI, despite its $157 billion valuation, is projected to lose $5 billion by September 2025. Anthropic, valued at $18 billion, has no clear path to profitability. The entire generative AI sector operates on what I call "profitability postponement": the belief that somehow, someday, the economics will work out.

This mirrors previous venture capital cycles that ended in tears. Uber, founded in 2009, still lost $1.8 billion in 2023, fourteen years after its founding. WeWork peaked at a $47 billion valuation before collapsing to near bankruptcy. Quibi raised $1.75 billion and shut down in six months. The playbook remains the same:

raise on hype, grow users at any cost, hope someone acquires you before the music stops.

The metrics shell game reveals the dysfunction. VC-funded companies have perfected the art of metric manipulation, replacing traditional business metrics (revenue, profit, cash flow) with growth theater: Monthly Active Users, regardless of monetization, Gross Merchandise Value that merely passes through their platforms, and Total Addressable Markets that exist only in pitch decks.

This creates the **VC Market Distortion Effect**. When VC-funded companies offer unsustainable pricing (ChatGPT at $20/month while losing money on every query, Google offering unlimited photo storage for free), they destroy the market for bootstrapped competitors who need to charge sustainable prices. Customers come to expect subsidized prices as "normal." Eventually, the VC company either raises prices dramatically, degrades service, or collapses entirely.

Contrast this with bootstrapped reality. Epic Systems charges hospitals millions for software that actually works. Mailchimp charged $10/month from the beginning. GitHub made developers pay for private repos. These companies didn't need to "figure out the business model later": the business model was the innovation. **This isn't innovation; it's speculation. Real innovation creates value that customers willingly pay for.**

The Capital Efficiency Calculator

Based on patterns from both historical and contemporary bootstrapped successes, I've developed the Capital Efficiency Calculator: a framework for evaluating whether bootstrapping is feasible for your innovation.

Revenue Potential Assessment

Factor	Bootstrappable	Requires VC
Time to Revenue	<6 months	>18 months
Initial Price Point	$10-1,000/month	$10,000+/month or free
Sales Complexity	Self-service	Enterprise sales cycle
Customer Acquisition	Product-led	Sales-led
Market Type	Existing demand	Market creation needed

Resource Requirement Analysis

Factor	Bootstrappable	Requires VC
Technical Complexity	Buildable by small team	Requires specialized experts
Infrastructure Needs	Cloud/SaaS	Physical infrastructure
Regulatory Requirements	Minimal	Heavy (FDA, FCC, etc.)
Time to Product	<6 months	>2 years
Capital Equipment	Software only	Hardware/ manufacturing

Competitive Dynamics Evaluation

Factor	Bootstrappable	Requires VC
Network Effects	Weak or product-based	Strong winner-take-all
Competition	Fragmented market	Race for dominance
Differentiation	Technical/product	Scale/network
Customer Lock-in	High switching costs	Low switching costs
Market Timing	Evergreen problem	Limited window

Score each factor. If you have >70% bootstrappable characteristics, you can likely bootstrap. 50-70% is marginal: consider starting bootstrapped and raising strategically later. <50% probably needs venture capital.

Key Insight: If you can reach profitability before running out of personal runway, you can bootstrap indefinitely.

When Venture Capital Actually Makes Sense

Despite my advocacy for bootstrapping, certain innovations genuinely require venture capital. Understanding these exceptions is as important as recognizing the bootstrap opportunity.

Winner-take-all markets represent the clearest case for VC. When network effects mean the first company to achieve critical mass wins everything, the speed that VC funding enables becomes essential. Facebook needed to dominate college campuses before competitors emerged. Uber needed to achieve liquidity in cities before regulators could react.

Regulatory capture opportunities, like Uber's need for massive capital to fight legal battles while establishing a presence, represent another valid use case. And sometimes markets have genuinely narrow windows (mobile app platforms in 2008, cryptocurrency in 2017, generative AI applications today) where speed to market determines everything.

The Bootstrap Reality Check

Before romanticizing the bootstrap path, let's be brutally honest about its challenges and limitations. The success stories I've shared (Mailchimp, Epic, Zoho) are exceptional precisely because they're exceptions.

The Privileges Often Unacknowledged

Financial runway: Mailchimp's founders could afford 8 years of consulting while building their product. Epic's Judy Faulkner had spousal income. WhatsApp's founders had Yahoo payouts. Most engineers don't have years of savings or spousal support to fund patient development.

Domain expertise: These founders had deep industry experience before starting. Mailchimp's founders understood email marketing. Epic's Faulkner had healthcare IT experience. Junior engineers or those changing industries lack this advantage.

Network access: Bootstrap success often requires customers willing to pay you before you're fully established. This requires professional networks that take years to build.

Market timing luck: Mailchimp launched in 2001 when email marketing was emerging, but not competitive. Epic started in 1979 when healthcare IT was nascent. Right timing, which is luck, not skill, played an enormous role.

When Bootstrap Is Genuinely Harder

Winner-take-all markets with funded competitors: If VC-funded competitors are achieving network effects, bootstrapping may mean losing by default.

Hardware with long development cycles: Bootstrapping a rocket company is effectively impossible. Some technical problems require capital-intensive infrastructure.

Regulated industries with high compliance costs: Achieving FDA approval for a new drug while bootstrap-funded is nearly impossible.

Markets requiring rapid land-grab: When being first matters more than being best, Bootstrap's patient pace becomes a liability.

Developing economies with less infrastructure: The bootstrap advice assumes access to profitable consulting markets, government grants, or revenue-based financing. These options may not exist in emerging economies.

The Failure Modes Nobody Discusses

Bootstrap burnout: Running unprofitably for years while consulting to survive is exhausting. Many bootstrap attempts fail not because the product was bad but because founders ran out of energy, savings, or family support.

Opportunity cost: The 5-10 years spent bootstrapping could have been spent working for a successful startup, gaining skills, building wealth, and networking, then starting with more resources.

Invisible failures: For every Mailchimp, hundreds of bootstrap attempts failed quietly. They never made tech blogs or conference talks.

The Third Path: Capital Stacking

For Deep Tech and hardware companies, a third path has emerged that deserves special attention: capital stacking. This approach blends multiple funding sources to survive the long development cycles that neither pure bootstrapping nor traditional VC can support.

Consider **Cellino Biotech**, winner of TechCrunch Disrupt 2021. Their technology (using AI and laser physics to automate stem cell manufacturing) required capital-intensive development that bootstrapping couldn't fund, but also required patient timelines that typical VC couldn't tolerate. Their solution: stack capital from multiple sources.

First, they raised $80 million Series A from Leaps by Bayer, 8VC, and Humboldt Fund. But they didn't stop there. In 2024, they secured a $25 million grant from ARPA-H (Advanced Research Projects Agency for Health) to develop their autonomous manufacturing system. Total funding: over $125 million, with a significant portion being non-dilutive government grants.

Minerva Lithium, a 2022 TechCrunch winner developing lithium extraction technology, followed a similar path: NSF SBIR grants, competition prize money, then targeted pilot programs, surviving the "valley of death" without massive VC dilution.

For engineers building hardware or deep tech, this hybrid approach offers a middle path: enough capital to build real technology, without the growth-at-all-costs pressure that destroys technical excellence. The key insight is that different capital sources optimize for different outcomes: VC for growth, grants for research, revenue for sustainability. Sophisticated founders blend them strategically.

Bootstrap vs VC Decision Framework

Question	If YES	If NO
Do you have 2-3 years financial runway?	Continue to next question	Consider VC or strategic funding
Do you have domain expertise to consult?	Continue to next question	Can you get alternative income?
Can reach profitability in 2-3 years?	Continue to next question	Need $1M+ upfront? → VC or hybrid
Is market winner-take-all?	VC or hybrid approach	BOOTSTRAP PATH
Capital intensive?	HYBRID: Grants/ RBF	BOOTSTRAP PATH

Decision Modifiers: Geographic location (consulting markets available?), competitive landscape (funded competitors?), technology type (software vs hardware vs deep tech), time sensitivity (land-grab moment?), risk tolerance (can you afford years of uncertainty?).

The Bootstrapper's Mindset

Bootstrapping isn't just a funding strategy. It's a philosophy that shapes everything about how you build. When customers fund you rather than VCs, you naturally optimize for customer value rather than investor metrics.

National Instruments exemplifies this philosophy. Founded in 1976 by three engineers with a $10,000 bank loan, they spent ten years developing LabVIEW: a graphical programming language that computer scientists mocked but engineers loved. They went public in 1995 with $179 million in revenue, having never taken venture capital. Today, they power everything from SpaceX rocket tests to CERN's Large Hadron Collider, with annual revenue exceeding $1.5 billion.

The bootstrapper's mindset embraces constraints as features. Small teams, as we'll see in Chapter 8, often force elegant simplicity rather than limiting it. Craigslist's refusal to modernize isn't stubbornness; it's understanding that complexity wouldn't improve the core value proposition.

Bootstrapping means never having to ask permission. No board approvals for product decisions. No investor updates explaining missed growth targets. No pressure to pivot when things don't immediately hockey-stick. Just you, your vision, and your customers: the only stakeholders who truly matter.

Conclusion: The Bootstrap Choice in Context

The venture capital industrial complex wants you to believe that VC funding is the only path to significant success. Current unicorn statistics seem to support this narrative. But statistics tell us what is, not what's possible.

The 94% of billion-dollar entrepreneurs who succeeded without early VC, whether in Rao's historical analysis or today's outliers like Mailchimp and Epic, prove that patient capital, customer funding, and technical excellence can beat venture capital. More importantly, they demonstrate that the bootstrap path often leads to better outcomes: founders retaining majority ownership, companies maintaining their vision, and innovations given time to mature properly.

For engineers, the implications are profound. You have unique advantages for bootstrapping that business founders lack. You can build products yourself. You can survive on minimal resources. You can create value directly without intermediaries. The Nordic innovation model, where government grants and patient capital support Deep Tech development, shows this isn't just an American phenomenon. Sweden ranks 2nd globally in innovation despite minimal VC activity compared to the US.

The bootstrap choice isn't about avoiding dilution or maintaining control, though these matter. It's about building the right way: sustainably, patiently, technically. It's about optimizing for customers rather than investors. It's about building companies that last rather than companies that exit.

It just requires the courage to build without permission.

References

1. Rao, D. (2019). Finance Secrets of Billion-Dollar Entrepreneurs. FIA Publications.
2. CB Insights. (2024). "The Complete List of Unicorn Companies." https://www.cbinsights.com/research-unicorn-companies
3. Chernev, B. (2021). "Mailchimp: From Side Project to $12 Billion Exit." Acquired Podcast, Episode 121.
4. Forbes. (2022). "Sara Blakely: The Spanx Success Story." Forbes Magazine.
5. Simon, H. (2009). Hidden Champions of the 21st Century: Success Strategies of Unknown World Market Leaders. Springer.
6. Ross, J., & Fonstad, N. (2022). "Forget Fail-Fast: Here's How to Master Digital Innovation." MIT Sloan Management Review, Winter 2022.
7. European Innovation Council. (2023). "EIC Accelerator Data: Capital Efficiency in Deep Tech." Statistical Report.
8. Thiel, P. (2014). Zero to One: Notes on Startups, or How to Build the Future. Crown Business.

CHAPTER 8

CONSTRAINTS AS FEATURES

The venture capital playbook assumes that more resources solve more problems. A common question reveals this mindset: "You're asking for $10 million, what could you do with $20 million? Could you develop faster?" The assumption is that capital and speed are linearly related.

But in hardware, constraints often are the solution. A robotics startup that can't afford a large team doesn't just make do with less; they're forced to automate what funded competitors staff. The result: a $10,000 robot instead of a $100,000 robot. Every person they don't hire becomes a system they have to build. Physics doesn't care about your burn rate. Some problems require sequential learning that no amount of parallel effort can accelerate.

Consider what this means at scale. In 2014, WhatsApp had around 55 employees. Facebook had over 6,300 employees. Google had 20,000. When Facebook acquired WhatsApp for $19 billion, those 55 employees were serving 450 million monthly users. Facebook, with its 6,300+ employees, served 1.2 billion users. WhatsApp was dramatically more efficient per person.

Resource scarcity, technical limitations, and artificial boundaries often produce better innovations than unlimited resources ever could. From Nintendo's "lateral thinking with withered technology" to China's Shanzhai innovation model, constraints don't limit innovation; they focus it. This is the engineer's secret weapon against better-funded competitors: turning poverty into power.

The IKEA Principle

In 1956, Ingvar Kamprad faced a problem that would reshape global retail. Customers were complaining about damaged furniture during delivery, and shipping costs were eating into profits. An employee removed the legs from a table to fit it into a car, and Kamprad had his epiphany: what if all furniture came unassembled?

This constraint (furniture must fit in a customer's car) seemed like a massive limitation. Competitors with delivery trucks laughed. But the constraint forced innovations that transformed IKEA into a $50 billion empire:

Constraint	Forced Innovation	Business Advantage
Furniture must be flat-packed	Pioneered modular design	30-50% lower prices
Customers assemble themselves	Mastered instruction design	No assembly labor costs
Everything must be flat	Warehouse efficiency	7x more inventory per space
Customers transport products	Outside city center locations	Cheap land costs

The constraint didn't hinder IKEA. It became their entire business model. Traditional furniture retailers still can't compete because their infrastructure assumes assembled furniture. They'd have to destroy their existing advantages (showrooms, delivery networks, assembly services) to copy IKEA's constraint-driven model.

This pattern appears everywhere once you start looking. 3M's Post-it Notes emerged from a "failed" adhesive that wasn't strong enough: the weakness became the feature. Twitter's 140-character limit, originally a technical constraint from SMS, forced a new form of communication that verbose platforms couldn't achieve. **The IKEA principle states: the most powerful innovations often come from embracing constraints rather than eliminating them.**

Nintendo's Philosophy: Lateral Thinking with Withered Technology

Gunpei Yokoi, the legendary Nintendo engineer who created the Game Boy, developed a philosophy that would define Nintendo's approach to innovation for decades: **"Lateral thinking with withered technology"** (枯れた技術の水平思考, *kareta gijutsu no suihei shikō*). Rather than pursuing cutting-edge technology, Yokoi advocated using mature, well-understood, inexpensive technology in novel ways.

The Game Boy exemplified this philosophy perfectly:

Feature	Game Boy	Competitors	Advantage
Screen	Monochrome	Color	30-hour vs 3-hour battery
Processor	1976 technology	Cutting-edge	Focus on gameplay over graphics
Price	$89	$179	Accessible to children's market
Durability	Indestructible	Fragile	Survived drops (crucial for kids)
Sales	118 million units	Crushed	Constraints became advantages

Yokoi's philosophy permeated Nintendo's culture. The Wii (2006) used motion sensors that were already in cars and smartphones, not cutting-edge technology. But Nintendo applied them laterally to gaming, creating a new category that outsold the technically superior PlayStation 3 and Xbox 360. The Nintendo DS used resistive touchscreens when capacitive was becoming standard, but resistive worked with styluses, enabling precision that finger-touch couldn't achieve.

As Yokoi explained in his 1997 book, The technology itself is not the important part. Using technology that has become cheap through mass production in a way that surprises people: that is the important part.

The Anti-Silicon Valley Startup

WhatsApp's story violates everything Silicon Valley teaches about scaling. No product managers. No growth team. No marketing department. No data scientists optimizing engagement. Just 55 employees building a messaging app that worked.

Constraint	Technical Solution	Result
Couldn't afford servers	Erlang: 2M connections/server	100x more efficient than Facebook
Couldn't afford marketing	$0.99 friction eliminated spam	Word-of-mouth growth
Couldn't afford large team	Automated via architecture	55 employees served 450M users
No moderation team	End-to-end encryption	No moderation needed by design
No account recovery team	Phone numbers as identities	Self-service identity

Every constraint forced a technical solution that turned out to be superior to the resource-intensive alternative. WhatsApp didn't succeed despite having only 55 employees: they succeeded because of it. A larger team would have built a more complex, less efficient system.

The $19 billion acquisition price worked out to $345 million per employee. This wasn't luck. It was the logical outcome of constraint-driven excellence.

DeepSeek: When Chip Embargoes Backfire

In late 2024, a Chinese AI lab called DeepSeek demonstrated something that surprised Silicon Valley: a model approaching GPT-4-level performance at a fraction of the cost. The twist? They did it without access to NVIDIA's latest H100 or H200 chips that Western labs consider essential. US export controls meant to constrain Chinese AI development had instead forced a breakthrough in efficiency.

The numbers are staggering. DeepSeek-V3, with 671 billion parameters, was trained for approximately $5.6 million, less than 5% of what comparable Western models cost. While OpenAI burns through billions in compute costs, DeepSeek achieved similar performance using older NVIDIA A100 chips and H800s (the export-compliant version with deliberately reduced interconnect speeds). The constraint of inferior hardware forced innovations that superior hardware would have made unnecessary.

How They Did It: The Technical Breakthroughs

Mixture-of-Experts (MoE) Architecture: Rather than activating all 671 billion parameters for every computation, DeepSeek routes each input to only the most relevant subset of expert networks. Think of it as having 671 specialists but only consulting the 37 who are relevant to your specific question. This reduces active computation by 95% while maintaining model quality.

Multi-head Latent Attention (MLA): Traditional transformer attention mechanisms create massive key-value caches that consume GPU memory exponentially as context length grows. DeepSeek's MLA compresses these caches by 75% through low-rank decomposition. With limited memory bandwidth on H800 chips, this compression was mandatory. For Western labs with H100s, it was never necessary to discover.

Extreme Quantization: DeepSeek pushed model weights from 16-bit precision down to 4-bit and even lower for certain layers, using sophisticated quantization-aware training that maintains accuracy. This 4x memory reduction lets them run larger models on smaller hardware.

Curriculum Learning at Scale: Rather than training on random data, DeepSeek carefully sequenced training examples from simple to complex, making each training token 2-3x more effective.

Each innovation individually seems modest. Combined, they multiply to achieve 20x efficiency gains. But here's what matters: none of these innovations would have emerged if DeepSeek had H100 access. The constraint of inferior chips forced algorithmic creativity that superior hardware would have rendered unnecessary.

DeepSeek published their techniques openly. They're not protecting trade secrets; they're demonstrating that assumed requirements for frontier AI may be more contingent than previously believed. Western AI labs' claims that frontier AI requires massive capital and cutting-edge hardware have been exposed as either ignorance or deliberate moat-building.

The constraint of chip embargoes didn't stop Chinese AI. It made it more dangerous to Western AI companies by proving their massive spending is unnecessary.

ISRO: Frugal Engineering in Space

India's space program offers perhaps the most dramatic demonstration of constraint-driven excellence. Operating on approximately one-tenth of NASA's budget, the Indian Space Research Organisation (ISRO) has achieved what should be impossible by Western standards.

In 2014, India's Mars Orbiter Mission (Mangalyaan) reached Mars orbit on its first attempt, a feat no other space agency had accomplished. The mission cost $74 million. NASA's comparable MAVEN mission to Mars cost $671 million. India achieved the same scientific objective for 11% of the cost. As one Indian space official noted, the Mars mission cost less than the Hollywood film "Gravity."

The constraint of limited funding forced engineering innovations that abundance never required:

Single-Version Engineering: While NASA builds multiple test versions before flight hardware, ISRO often builds a single "flight-quality" version from the start. This forces extreme care in design but eliminates the cost of duplicate hardware.

Gravity Assist Trajectories: Unable to afford more powerful rockets, ISRO developed expertise in complex orbital mechanics, using the moon's gravity as a slingshot to reach Mars with less fuel. What seemed like a limitation became a demonstration of navigational sophistication.

Component Reuse: ISRO's Chandrayaan-3, which achieved the first-ever lunar south pole landing in 2023 for just $75 million, reused components from previous missions rather than designing from scratch. Frugality drove modularity.

The Shanzhai Innovation Model: Creativity Through Copying

China's Shanzhai (山寨) phenomenon offers a radically different perspective on constraint-driven innovation. Originally referring to mountain strongholds outside government control, Shanzhai came to describe the underground factories in Shenzhen producing unauthorized copies of branded products. Western observers dismissed it as mere piracy. They missed the innovation hidden within the copying.

Shanzhai manufacturers faced extreme constraints: no access to official components, no brand recognition, minimal capital, and constant legal threats. These constraints forced remarkable innovations. Shanzhai phones weren't just cheap iPhone copies: they were entirely different products serving different needs.

Shanzhai phones pioneered dual-SIM functionality years before major brands, recognizing that poor users needed to switch between carriers for the best rates. They added features branded phones ignored: massive speakers for construction workers, waterproofing for farmers, and week-long battery life for areas with unreliable electricity. Some included cigarette lighters, portable TVs, and even Geiger counters. They served customers that Apple and Samsung literally couldn't see.

Many legitimate Chinese tech giants emerged from Shanzhai roots. Xiaomi started by studying Shanzhai's rapid iteration model. Huawei's early phones borrowed heavily from Shanzhai innovations. The constraint of being outside the system forced a creativity that being inside would have prevented.

Modern Constraint Victories: Three Case Studies

Raspberry Pi: The $35 Computer Revolution

In 2012, Eben Upton faced a crisis in computer science education. Fewer British students were applying to Cambridge's CS program, and those who did lacked programming experience. Modern PCs were too expensive and too complex for children to experiment with fearlessly.

Upton's constraint was brutal: create a complete computer for under $35, less than 5% of what education-focused computers typically cost. This forced radical innovation: strip everything to bare essentials, use a mobile phone processor (ARM chips had become cheap through smartphone volume), eliminate all peripherals except USB and HDMI, make it so cheap that breaking one wouldn't matter.

The Raspberry Pi was shipped in 2012 for exactly $35. By 2024, over 50 million units will have been sold. NASA uses Raspberry Pis on the International Space Station. CERN uses them for sensor networks. The constraint of extreme affordability enabled use cases that "proper" computers, at 10x the cost, could never serve.

Starlink: When Physics Becomes Product

SpaceX's Starlink faced a constraint that defeated previous satellite internet attempts: the laws of physics. Traditional satellite internet used geostationary satellites at 36,000 km altitude, far enough that latency (~600ms) made real-time applications impossible.

SpaceX couldn't change the speed of light. But they could change the altitude. By placing satellites in low Earth orbit (550 km instead of 36,000 km), Starlink reduced minimum latency to ~20-40ms, competitive with ground-based internet. But this created new constraints: satellites at 550 km orbit Earth every

90 minutes (not geostationary), requiring thousands of satellites instead of dozens.

These new constraints forced innovations that traditional satellite companies would never have discovered. Starlink pioneered mass production of satellites (currently launching 40+ per month), automated orbital coordination for thousands of satellites, and phased-array antennas that track satellites as they race overhead. The physics constraint of latency was transformed into a massive constellation advantage.

RISC-V: The Open Architecture Insurgency

For decades, processor design meant licensing ARM or x86 architectures, paying royalties on every chip. This constraint limited who could innovate in processor design. Universities couldn't afford licensing fees for research. Startups couldn't risk building on architectures where the licensor might become a competitor.

In 2010, UC Berkeley professors faced this constraint directly: they wanted to research processor design but couldn't afford ARM licenses, and x86 was too complex. Their solution: create a completely open, royalty-free instruction set architecture called RISC-V. The constraint of zero budget forced simplicity. RISC-V's base integer instruction set has just 47 instructions versus hundreds for x86.

What started as a workaround for academic licensing costs has exploded into an ecosystem threat to ARM and Intel. RISC-V implementations now come from Google, NVIDIA, Qualcomm, and hundreds of startups. China has adopted RISC-V as a strategic response to US chip restrictions. The constraint of proprietary architecture costs didn't just create an alternative. It created a fundamentally different innovation model where anyone can design processors without permission or royalties.

Each case follows the same pattern: a constraint that seems insurmountable (price, physics, intellectual property) gets transformed into a design principle that creates advantages unavailable to unconstrained competitors.

The Next Constraint: Circular Design

The most powerful constraints are often those that haven't fully materialized yet. Circular economy design represents exactly this: a constraint that's transforming from an optional sustainability initiative to a fundamental design requirement.

Three converging forces are making linear design (extract, manufacture, use, dispose) increasingly unviable:

Regulatory Pressure: The EU's Circular Economy Action Plan now mandates design-for-disassembly, right-to-repair, and extended producer responsibility. By 2030, products that can't be repaired, refurbished, or recycled will face market restrictions or disposal taxes.

Resource Scarcity: Critical materials for electronics (rare earth elements, lithium, cobalt) face supply constraints. Redwood Materials, founded by Tesla co-founder JB Straubel, recovers 95%+ of battery materials and has become the largest "cobalt miner" in the United States without operating a single mine.

Cost Economics: Circular design often reduces production costs. When IKEA designed products for disassembly, they discovered that modular design reduced manufacturing complexity. When Philips created lighting-as-a-service (keeping ownership of bulbs to recycle materials), they found servitization created better margins than product sales.

Framework and Fairphone: Proving the Impossible

Framework Laptop: Every component is user-replaceable, from RAM to motherboard to ports. The constraint of designing a laptop that customers can upgrade for a decade forced innovations: a swappable expansion card system ($9 to upgrade USB 3 to USB 4), a mainboard marketplace, QR-coded parts with repair documentation, and open-source schematics.

Fairphone: In 2013, conventional wisdom said smartphones couldn't be modular and repairable. Fairphone proved this was a choice, not physics. Their phones achieve IP55 water resistance with user-replaceable batteries, screens, cameras, and charging ports. No glue, no soldering. The constraint of repairability forced 8 years of software updates (vs 2-3 for most Android) and unprecedented supply chain transparency.

Apple and Dell can't easily copy these approaches because their entire supply chain and design philosophy optimize for sealed, unrepairable products. The circular constraint became a competitive moat.

Craigslist: The $5 Billion Zen Garden

Craig Newmark started Craigslist in 1995 as an email list for San Francisco events. At its peak, it was estimated to generate over $1 billion in revenue with roughly 50 employees, more than $20 million per employee, possibly the highest revenue-per-employee ratio of any major internet company.

Even after years of decline from competitors like Facebook Marketplace and OfferUp, Craigslist still generates an estimated $300 million annually with the same tiny team. That's still roughly $6 million per employee, a ratio most venture-backed startups never achieve.

Everything about Craigslist seems wrong. The design has

remained unchanged since 1996. It appears to be a computer science student's first HTML project. No images on the homepage. No JavaScript frameworks. No mobile app for years. No recommendation algorithm. No social features.

Yet Craigslist destroyed newspaper classified revenues: a $20 billion industry. It remains the number one U.S. classified site by traffic despite countless competitors with superior technology, design, and funding. Why?

The constraints are the product. Because Craigslist refuses to modernize, pages load instantly even on slow connections. Because there's no algorithm, there's no filter bubble; you see everything chronologically. Because there's no venture capital, there's no pressure to extract maximum revenue. Craig Newmark still owns the company and runs it like a public service that happens to make money.

Competitors consistently fail because they remove the constraints that make Craigslist work. They add features, algorithms, and optimizations that make the experience worse. Craigslist proves that sometimes the best feature is the absence of features.

The Constraint Innovation Matrix

Type of Constraint	What It Forces	Innovation Outcome	Example
Resource Constraints	Efficiency and code elegance	Superior performance per resource	WhatsApp: 55 employees = 450M users
Time Constraints	Focus on core, ruthless cutting	Simplified but powerful products	MVP mindset: Ship core only
Technical Constraints	Creative workarounds	Novel solutions become features	Nintendo: Withered tech → Game Boy
Hardware Constraints	Algorithmic innovation	Efficiency breakthroughs	DeepSeek: Chip embargo → 5% cost
Regulatory Constraints	Innovation arbitrage	New categories before rules	Uber operated before regulations
Cultural Constraints	Forced creativity	Unexpected innovations	Shanzhai: No IP → open hardware
Self-Imposed Constraints	Philosophical clarity	Breakthrough simplicity	Apple's "no stylus" → multitouch

Key Insight: Constraints aren't obstacles to innovation: they're catalysts for it. The question isn't "How do we get more resources?" but "How do we use constraints as design principles?"

The Constraint Discipline Toolkit

Constraint Mapping: List every resource you lack that competitors have. For each constraint, ask: "What if this were permanent? How would we succeed anyway?" This mental exercise reveals non-obvious solutions.

Forced Ranking: With unlimited resources, everything seems important. Constraints force brutal prioritization. Rank every feature, hire, and expense. Cut the bottom 80%. What remains is your true core.

Constraint Arbitrage: Find resources others waste. WhatsApp used Erlang: a language most ignored. Craigslist used simple HTML when everyone chased rich interfaces. Arduino used open-source when everyone protected IP.

Lateral Application: Following Yokoi's philosophy, identify mature technologies in other industries. How could "withered technology" from automotive, aerospace, or medical fields revolutionize your domain?

Efficiency Metrics: Track unusual ratios: users per engineer, revenue per server, features per line of code. Optimize for efficiency, not absolute numbers. Small teams that measure efficiency often outperform large teams that measure output.

Conclusion: The Power of Less

The myth of Silicon Valley is that innovation requires abundant resources: venture capital, large teams, expensive infrastructure. The reality revealed by Nintendo, IKEA, Shanzhai, and DeepSeek is that constraints breed better innovations than abundance.

This isn't an argument for artificial poverty or intentional limitation. It's recognition that resource constraints force clarity, efficiency, and creativity that abundance obscures. When you can't throw money at problems, you have to think. When you can't hire your way to solutions, you have to innovate. When you can't access the latest hardware, as DeepSeek proved, you have to discover algorithmic breakthroughs that make hardware advantages irrelevant.

The DeepSeek revelation in December 2024 may mark a turning point in how we understand innovation. When a Chinese team working under chip embargoes can match OpenAI's performance at 5% of the cost, it exposes the wastefulness of resource-abundant innovation. Every Western AI company claiming they need billions more in funding has been proven wrong by engineers who had neither.

For engineers, this is liberating. You don't need Google's resources to compete with Google. You don't need NVIDIA's latest chips to compete with OpenAI. You need constraints that force innovations your better-funded competitors would never discover. Your 5-person team isn't a limitation. It's an advantage that forces efficiency their 500-person team can't achieve.

Every resource constraint is also a clarity constraint. Less money means clearer priorities. Fewer people mean better communication. Less time means focused execution. Inferior hardware means superior algorithms.

Constraints aren't obstacles. They're specifications.

As Gunpei Yokoi proved with the Game Boy, and as DeepSeek proved with AI, the future often belongs not to those with the most advanced technology, but to those who use simple technology in the most advanced ways.

But constraints do more than force creative solutions; they force something even more valuable: revenue. When you can't raise millions, you must sell. When you can't hire, you must automate. The ultimate constraint-driven innovation isn't technical. It's financial.

References

1. Yokoi, G., & Makino, T. (1997). Yokoi Gunpei Game House. ASCII Corporation.
2. Keane, M. (2007). Created in China: The Great New Leap Forward. Routledge.
3. Lindtner, S. (2020). Prototype Nation: China and the Contested Promise of Innovation. Princeton University Press.
4. Simon, H. (2009). Hidden Champions of the 21st Century: Success Strategies of Unknown World Market Leaders. Springer.
5. European Small Business Journal. (2019). "Resource Constraints and Radical Innovation: A Meta-Analysis." Vol. 37, Issue 4.
6. DeepSeek. (2024). "DeepSeek-V3 Technical Report." arXiv:2412.19437, December 2024.
7. Financial Times. (2025). "How DeepSeek's AI Breakthrough Challenges Silicon Valley's Assumptions." January 2025.

CHAPTER 9

THE REVENUE PATH

Atlassian reached $59 million in annual revenue before raising any venture capital. Basecamp has generated over $100 million annually while staying completely bootstrapped. Epic Systems handles medical records for approximately 75% of Americans without ever taking outside investment. The pattern is consistent: they all started by selling services before building products. They got customers to fund their product development by solving immediate problems first.

The survivorship caveat: For every Atlassian or Basecamp, hundreds of consulting companies never successfully made the transition to products. Many get trapped in the consulting trap, where high-margin services consume all resources, leaving no capacity for product development. The revenue path works, but it requires disciplined resource allocation and knowing when to say no to lucrative consulting work.

Yet walk into any startup accelerator and suggest beginning with consulting work, and you'll hear the same objections: "That doesn't scale." "You'll get distracted from the product vision." "Real startups raise capital, not revenue." This disconnect between what demonstrably works and what we teach reveals the innovation establishment's deepest blind spot: the belief that venture capital is the only legitimate path to building breakthrough products.

The persistent myth is that innovation requires burning money before making it. This myth endures because venture capitalists need it to be true. Their entire model depends on companies needing capital before revenue. But engineers who've successfully built billion-dollar companies know a secret: customers will pay you to build your product if you structure the journey correctly.

Revenue-first innovation isn't just bootstrapping through consulting. It's architecting your entire innovation path so that each stage generates revenue that funds the next stage. From Atlassian's evolution from consulting to $60 billion SaaS giant, to the European Deep Tech companies using customer contracts to compete with Silicon Valley, the evidence is clear: revenue is the best funding. Getting paid to discover what others spend millions to guess is the engineer's ultimate arbitrage.

The Service Layer Strategy

Before examining specific tactics, we need to understand a pattern hidden in plain sight: most successful technical products have a service layer in their history that their founders rarely discuss. This isn't embarrassing prehistory. It's the foundation that made everything else possible.

Palantir, now worth $50 billion, spent its first five years as essentially a consulting company. They'd send teams of engineers to work directly with CIA analysts, building custom data analysis tools. Each deployment taught them what intelligence analysts actually needed versus what they said they needed. By the time they productized Palantir Gotham, they'd been paid millions to discover exactly what to build.

Unity Technologies followed a similar pattern. Before becoming the game engine powering half of all mobile games, they started as Over the Edge Entertainment, building their own games while developing the Unity engine. They extracted reusable components with each project, eventually realizing the engine was more valuable than the games. When they pivoted to selling the engine, they knew exactly what game developers needed because they'd been game developers. Their game development work hadn't been a distraction from building a product; it had been essential research they were paid to conduct.

ASML, now the world's monopoly supplier of extreme ultraviolet lithography machines worth €300 billion, built deep customer relationships through years of collaborative development with chipmakers. Each project taught them what the industry needed, funded R&D, and built relationships that would become their moat.

These companies didn't pivot from services to products: they evolved. The service work wasn't a temporary survival strategy but the foundation of deep domain knowledge that made their products successful.

Traditional Path vs. Service Layer Path

Traditional Path	Service Layer Path
Guess what to build	Find customers with problems
Raise money	Get paid to solve specific instances
Build product	Extract patterns
Find customers	Productize patterns
Iterate toward product-market fit	Sell product to service customers

The service path seems longer, but it's actually faster to real product-market fit because you're not guessing. Every feature in your product exists because a customer paid you to build it.

A critical distinction: The Service Layer Strategy is not customer validation in disguise. In traditional customer development, you validate market desire through interviews, surveys, and sticky notes. In the Service Layer, you validate utility through engineering contracts and paid deliverables. One gathers data about hypothetical demand; the other generates revenue from demonstrated capability.

Atlassian: The $60 Billion Evolution

Atlassian's journey from consulting to product exemplifies the revenue path perfectly. Mike Cannon-Brookes and Scott Farquhar started in 2002 with a $10,000 credit card advance, initially building websites and custom Java applications for clients. They weren't trying to build a product company; they just wanted to avoid getting "real jobs."

Through their consulting work, they noticed every client needed similar tools: bug tracking, project management, and knowledge bases. Instead of building these from scratch each time, they created reusable components. Jira started as their internal bug tracker, which they began installing for clients. Confluence emerged from the wiki systems they'd built multiple times.

The crucial insight: they didn't stop consulting when they started selling products. For years, they operated a hybrid model where product sales were supplemented by implementation services. This gave them deep customer relationships, steady revenue, and constant feedback on what features to build next.

By maintaining the service layer while building products, Atlassian achieved something remarkable: it reached $100 million in revenue without a single salesperson. How? Their service relationships became their sales channel. Every consulting client became a product customer. Every product customer referred them to other companies facing similar problems.

The numbers tell the story: $320 million revenue at IPO in 2015, 60% EBITDA margins, 48,000 customers, zero venture capital until going public. Today they're worth over $60 billion, with the founders still owning 30% each. The service-to-product evolution didn't slow them down. It de-risked everything.

The Revenue Evolution Pathway

Based on patterns from successful technical founders across multiple continents, I've developed the Revenue Evolution Pathway: a systematic approach to evolving from trading time for money to building scalable products.

Stage	Model	Description	Risk Eliminated
1. Pure Consulting	Time for money	Solve problems with your expertise. Choose work aligned with eventual product vision.	Problem space discovery
2. Productized Consulting	Fixed-fee projects	Package solutions: "$25,000 to integrate your payment system" instead of hourly billing. Forces systematization.	Solution repeatability
3. Hybrid Service	Tools + expertise	Blend automated tools with human expertise. Monthly fee for tools plus support.	Automation viability
4. Product + Services	Product core, services edge	Product handles 80% of use cases; paid services for customization and onboarding.	Market acceptance
5. Pure Product	Self-service SaaS	Fully automated, services optional. The promised land, but you arrived with customers, revenue, and domain expertise.	Scale readiness

Buildkite exemplifies this evolution. The founders started as DevOps consultants in Melbourne, helping companies with continuous integration. They built custom CI/CD pipelines for each client (Stage 1), then created reusable scripts and tools (Stage 2), then offered "CI/CD as a Service" with their tools (Stage 3), then launched Buildkite as a product with professional services (Stage 4), and finally achieved pure self-service SaaS (Stage 5). They reached significant revenue without taking venture capital until their Series A in 2018.

Each stage de-risks the next. Consulting proves demand exists. Productized consulting proves you can systematize solutions. Hybrid models prove customers will pay for automation. By the time you reach pure product, you've eliminated most market risk.

Government Grants: The Hidden Billions

While Silicon Valley obsesses over venture capital, governments worldwide pour billions into innovation through non-dilutive grants. These programs are specifically designed for the kind of patient and technical innovation that engineers excel at.

In the United States, the SBIR/STTR programs distribute $3.5 billion annually across 11 federal agencies. Unlike VC funding, you keep 100% equity. Unlike revenue, you don't need customers yet. The catch? You need to solve problems the government cares about, which covers nearly every field from robotics to biotechnology to quantum computing.

SBIR/STTR Three-Phase Structure

Phase	Funding	Duration	Purpose
Phase I	$50k-275k	6-12 months	Prove feasibility
Phase II	$750k-1.5M	2 years	Build prototypes
Phase III	Unlimited	Ongoing	Government contracts for deployment

Qualcomm, Symantec, and iRobot all used SBIR funding in their early days. Modern examples include Boston Dynamics (DARPA funding for decades before commercial products) and Moderna (DARPA funding for mRNA platform development).

The European Innovation Council has become even more aggressive, offering up to €17.5 million per company: €2.5 million in grants plus €15 million in equity investment. Unlike US programs, the EIC actively helps companies commercialize beyond government contracts. Deep Tech companies across Europe have received substantial funding through various EU programs to develop fusion energy, quantum computing, and other long-term technologies. This patient capital would be impossible to secure from VCs, given the 20+ year timelines involved.

China's approach differs but is equally substantial. The government provides massive support for strategic technologies through subsidies and guaranteed government purchases. BYD's battery development benefited from extensive government support and contracts that funded their R&D. This patient capital allowed them to spend over a decade perfecting lithium iron phosphate batteries while Tesla was still using Panasonic's cells.

Key Insight: Governments might fund innovation that VCs won't touch. Anything with 10+ year development cycles, massive capital requirements, or strategic importance has a government program. You just need to know where to look.

Revenue-Based Financing: The Optimal Middle Path

Between bootstrapping and venture capital lies an option gaining global traction: revenue-based financing (RBF). Instead of selling equity, you sell a percentage of future revenues until the investor receives a predetermined return (typically 1.5-3x their investment).

The mechanics are elegantly simple. An RBF firm invests $1 million with a 2x cap. You pay them 5% of monthly revenues until they've received $2 million. If you grow quickly, you get paid back quickly. If you grow slowly, they wait. But crucially, you keep all equity and control.

This model has exploded globally. In the US, Pipe has institutionalized trading future revenues for present capital. In Europe, Uncapped and Outfund provide similar models. In India, GetVantage funds hundreds of companies. In Africa, GreenTec Capital uses RBF to fund sustainable tech. The model works because it aligns incentives: investors want you to generate sustainable revenue, not achieve unicorn valuations.

For engineers, RBF offers something VCs can't: patience for technical excellence. RBF investors are happy with steady 30% annual growth that VCs would consider failure. This patience allows you to build technical moats rather than chase growth metrics. You're optimizing for sustainable revenue, not explosive growth that often breaks the product.

Customer-Funded Development: The Ultimate Validation

The ultimate revenue-first strategy is getting customers to pay for development upfront. This isn't theoretical. It's how most aerospace and defense innovation happens. Lockheed Martin doesn't build fighter jets hoping someone will buy them. They get multi-billion-dollar development contracts first.

This model is increasingly accessible to small companies. Enterprises tired of waiting for vendors to build features will pay for accelerated development. Government agencies will fund specific capabilities they need. Even other startups will pay for integrations that unlock their own growth.

Red Hat mastered this model before its $34 billion IBM acquisition. Large enterprises would pay them millions to add specific features to Red Hat Enterprise Linux. Red Hat would build the feature, keep the IP, and sell it to everyone else. Customers got what they needed immediately; Red Hat got paid for R&D that benefited all customers.

The **German Mittelstand** companies have perfected customer-funded innovation. Companies like Trumpf, a world leader in laser cutting machines with €4.2 billion in revenue, develop new technologies in close partnership with industrial customers who need cutting-edge capabilities. Automotive manufacturers fund the development of lasers for new materials and applications; that R&D then benefits all Trumpf customers. This collaborative development model has made Germany's hidden champions dominant in their industrial niches.

The key to customer-funded development:

Principle	Why It Matters
You retain all intellectual property rights	Future customers benefit from past development
Features become part of your standard product	Development compounds across customer base
Customer gets early access or discounted rates	Fair exchange for funding risk
Development timeline aligns with customer needs	Both parties win
Clear specifications prevent scope creep	Protects both sides

This model is particularly powerful for platform companies. Each customer-funded integration makes your platform more valuable for all customers. You're essentially getting paid to increase your network effects.

The Funding Decision Framework

Given these options, how do you choose? Here's a framework based on successful patterns across different regions and industries:

Your Situation	Recommended Path	Rationale
Zero Revenue		
Can consult in your domain	Service Layer Strategy	Get paid to learn the problem space
Deep Tech with long timeline	Government Grants (SBIR/EIC)	Patient capital for patient innovation
Have potential anchor customer	Customer-Funded Development	De-risk with committed buyer
Must capture market immediately	Consider VC (understand the tradeoffs)	Speed sometimes matters more than ownership
Early Revenue ($1-100k/month)		
Predictable SaaS revenue	Revenue-Based Financing	Non-dilutive growth capital
Enterprise customers	Customer-Funded Development	Let big customers fund features
Growing 20%+ monthly	Keep bootstrapping	Don't fix what isn't broken
Need R&D capital	Government grants + revenue	Combine funding sources

Your Situation	Recommended Path	Rationale
Scaling Revenue ($100k+/month)		
Need growth capital	RBF or strategic Series A	Choose based on market dynamics
Winner-take-all market	VC (but on your terms)	Sometimes you need to move fast
Building Deep Tech moat	Government grants + revenue	Patient capital for patient moats
Sustainable growth	Stay independent	Why dilute if you don't have to?

The crucial realization: These aren't mutually exclusive. Successful companies combine multiple approaches. SpaceX used NASA contracts (customer funding) plus private investment. BioNTech used German government grants plus eventual VC funding. Basecamp used consulting revenue plus eventual profits to stay independent forever.

Conclusion: The Customer-Funded Future

The innovation ecosystem has created a false binary: either bootstrap slowly or take VC and grow fast. But engineers who build lasting companies know there's a third way: let customers fund your innovation.

Whether through service layers that evolve into products, government grants for deep tech, revenue-based financing for growth, or development contracts from enterprise customers, the options for non-dilutive funding have never been better. The European model of patient capital through grants, the Asian model of customer-funded development, and the emerging global RBF ecosystem all point to the same conclusion: you don't need to sell your company to build it.

Every dollar of revenue is worth more than ten dollars

of investment. Revenue validates market demand, funds development, and maintains your independence. Investment might accelerate growth, but revenue ensures survival.

The path from service to product, from consulting to SaaS, from custom to scalable, isn't a compromise. It's a strategy. You're not delaying your product vision; you're getting paid to refine it. You're not distracted by services; you're learning exactly what to build.

For engineers, this approach leverages our natural strengths. We solve real problems for real customers. We build what's needed, not what might be wanted. We generate value immediately, not eventually. Most importantly, we maintain control of our innovations rather than becoming employees of our investors.

Revenue isn't the opposite of innovation. It's the proof of it.

Revenue funds development. But the ultimate expression of this principle is building platforms. This is the ultimate engineer's leverage: creating infrastructure that others pay to use, funding your growth while teaching you exactly what to build next.

References

1. European Innovation Council. (2024). "EIC Accelerator Guide for Applicants." European Commission.
2. Hathaway, I. (2023). "Revenue-Based Financing: A New Way Forward." Kauffman Foundation Research.
3. National Institute of Standards and Technology. (2024). "SBIR/STTR America's Seed Fund Powered by SBA." NIST.gov.
4. Simon, H. (2009). Hidden Champions of the 21st Century. Springer.
5. Pipe Technologies. (2023). "The State of Revenue-Based Financing Report."

CHAPTER 10

THE PLATFORM PLAY

In 2003, Amazon was bleeding money on infrastructure. Every holiday season brought server crashes and angry customers. The engineering team had built sophisticated systems to handle traffic spikes, but most of this capacity sat idle for eleven months of the year. At an executive retreat, Andy Jassy posed what seemed like an absurd question: "What if we sold our excess computing capacity to others?"

The room went silent. Amazon sold books. Then DVDs. Then everything. But computing power? That wasn't a product; it was infrastructure. Infrastructure was a cost, not revenue. Infrastructure was what you built so you could sell actual things.

The platform play is the engineer's ultimate leverage move, one that MBAs rarely understand. Platforms don't solve specific problems; they enable others to solve problems you haven't imagined. They don't serve users; they create ecosystems. Engineers build platforms while business people build products because engineers see infrastructure as capability, not cost.

AWS: The Platform Built for Itself

AWS was not built without business intent, but it was built without a validated market for what it would eventually become. Its origin story reveals how platforms emerge, not through upfront strategic planning, but by solving internal problems at scale. By 2002, Amazon's engineering teams were drowning in redundancy. Every team was building its own databases, storage systems, and computing infrastructure.

Bezos's API Mandate

#	Rule
1	All teams must expose data and functionality through service interfaces
2	Teams must communicate only through these interfaces
3	No direct database access, no shared memory, no backdoors
4	All interfaces must be designed as if exposed to external developers
5	Anyone who doesn't follow this will be fired

The crucial insight: Bezos wasn't thinking about creating a cloud computing platform. He was solving an internal systems problem. But by forcing every team to build as if external developers would use their services, he accidentally created the architecture for AWS.

The first AWS service, Simple Queue Service (SQS), launched in 2004. Amazon did something unprecedented: they sold infrastructure as a service to anyone. No contracts, no minimums, no sales calls. Just APIs and credit cards.

The reaction from established technology companies was dismissive. Larry Ellison called cloud computing "gibberish." Microsoft's Steve Ballmer laughed at the idea of retailers selling computing. IBM executives couldn't understand why anyone would trust critical infrastructure to a bookstore.

Aspect	Before AWS	After AWS
Getting servers	Raise money, wait weeks	Type command, servers appear
Scaling	Capacity planning as existential risk	Scale up/down automatically
Payment	Large capital upfront	Pay only for what you use
Infrastructure	Physical data centers	Infrastructure becomes code

AWS succeeded not by being better infrastructure but by being *programmable* infrastructure. EC2 instances weren't faster than dedicated servers. S3 wasn't more reliable than SANs. But you could provision them with code, orchestrate them with APIs, and scale them with algorithms. Infrastructure became software, and software eats everything.

Alibaba's Platform Evolution: From Marketplace to Ecosystem

While Amazon was building cloud infrastructure, Jack Ma was solving a different problem in China: trust. In 2003, Chinese consumers didn't trust online sellers, sellers didn't trust buyers, and nobody trusted online payments. Taobao, Alibaba's answer to eBay, didn't just create a marketplace; it built an entire trust infrastructure that became a platform ecosystem.

As Ming Zeng, Alibaba's Chief Strategy Officer, wrote in *Smart Business*, Alibaba's vision evolved from being "an e-commerce company" to one where "we aim to build the future infrastructure of commerce."

Alipay (2004): Started as an escrow service for Taobao. Buyers paid Alipay, which held funds until delivery confirmation. This solved the trust problem but created a platform for all online payments, eventually becoming Ant Financial.

Cainiao (2013): Instead of building logistics like Amazon, Alibaba created a data platform connecting thousands of logistics companies. The platform optimizes routing across competitors, creating efficiency that no single company could achieve.

Alibaba Cloud (2009): Like AWS, it started serving internal needs but evolved differently, specializing in retail and finance infrastructure, and offering not just servers but complete business solutions.

The pattern differs from Western platforms: Alibaba doesn't just provide tools; it orchestrates entire value chains. When a merchant joins Taobao, they get access to payments, logistics, cloud computing, financing, and marketing, all integrated through Alibaba's platform.

Samsung's Chaebol Platform: Vertical Integration as Ecosystem

South Korea's Samsung represents a completely different platform approach, the chaebol model, where vertical integration creates internal platforms. Samsung doesn't just make phones; it makes the screens, processors, memory, and batteries inside them, and sells these components to competitors.

This creates a unique platform dynamic:

Internal Customer Platform: Samsung's component divisions must compete for both internal customers (Samsung Mobile) and external ones (Apple). This forces world-class quality; Apple won't accept inferior screens just because Samsung makes them.

Technology Transfer Platform: Innovations in one division become platforms for others. OLED technology developed for TVs becomes smartphone screens. Battery technology from laptops powers electric vehicles.

Manufacturing Platform: Samsung's foundries produce chips for competitors using Samsung's process technology. They're simultaneously competing with and enabling rivals.

Scale Economics Platform: By serving both internal needs and external customers, Samsung achieves scale no pure-play company can match, enabling R&D investments others can't justify, like spending $15 billion annually on semiconductor development.

The chaebol model shows that platforms don't require openness; they require systematic capability building that others can leverage, whether internal divisions or external customers.

The Arduino Revolution: Democratizing Hardware

While Amazon was turning servers into services, Massimo Banzi was teaching interaction design in Italy, facing a different problem. His students needed to prototype electronic projects, but microcontroller boards cost hundreds of dollars and required electrical engineering degrees to program. In 2005, Banzi created Arduino: a $30 board that artists could program.

The design decisions that made Arduino a platform reveal systems thinking at its finest:

Open Hardware: Designs, schematics, and PCB layouts released under Creative Commons. Anyone could manufacture Arduino-compatible boards. This seemed like business suicide, but it created an ecosystem where innovation happened at the edges, not the center.

Simple Programming Model: Arduino's IDE and simplified C++ hid the complexity that had gatekept hardware development. Professional engineers mocked it as "toy programming." But simplicity enabled complexity, when everyone can prototype, more prototypes become products.

Standardized Shields: The brilliant insight was standardizing expansion connectors. Anyone could build "shields" that stacked on top, motor controllers, wireless modules, and sensor arrays. No negotiation, no licensing, no permission needed.

Community-Driven Libraries: Instead of supporting every sensor, Arduino provided a framework for community libraries. Someone in Japan could write a library for a specific sensor, and someone in Brazil could use it the next day.

Arduino didn't compete on specifications. Professional boards had faster processors, more memory, and better debugging. Arduino won by being a platform that enabled an ecosystem.

ROS: The Robot Operating System That Isn't

The story of Robot Operating System (ROS) represents perhaps the purest platform play in technology history. In 2007, robotics was fragmented into incompatible silos. Every research lab rebuilt basic functionality, including motor control, sensor processing, and navigation algorithms. PhD students spent years reimplementing known solutions instead of advancing the field.

Willow Garage, funded by early Google employee Scott Hassan, decided to build robot infrastructure rather than better robots. ROS wasn't actually an operating system; it was a communication framework that let robot components talk to each other.

Distributed by Design: ROS treated every sensor, actuator, and algorithm as a node that published and subscribed to messages. Everything is loosely coupled through message passing.

Language Agnostic: Nodes could be written in Python, C++, Java, or any language that could serialize messages. The platform didn't care about implementation, only interfaces.

Simulation-First Development: ROS integrated with physics simulators from day one. Develop robot behaviors in simulation, deploy to hardware without changing code.

Package Management: ROS introduced apt-style package management to robotics, turning the installation of complex capabilities, like a full SLAM stack, into a one-line command.

By 2025, ROS had grown far beyond academia: it underpinned research, startups, and space-grade robotic systems such as NASA's Astrobee, and it influenced how companies approached logistics and automation prototyping. Still, ROS never became the universal control layer for factory automation, major fulfillment centers, or surgical suites; its impact was profound, but not all-encompassing.

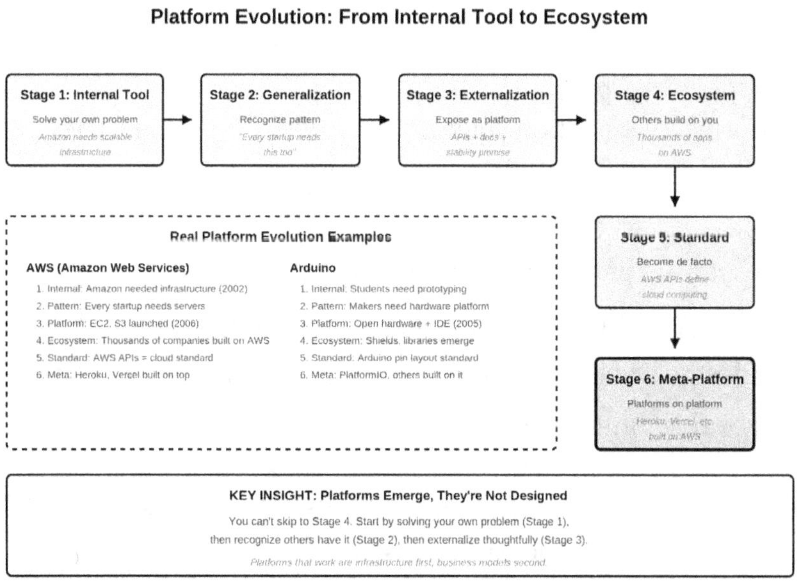

Platform Evolution: From Internal Tool to Ecosystem

Based on these patterns, platforms emerge and evolve through predictable stages:

Stage	Description	Example	Key Metric
1. Internal Tool	Build to solve your own problem	Amazon's internal compute	0 external users
2. Pattern Recognition	Realize others have same problem	"Every startup needs servers"	Problem validated
3. Platform Exposure	Expose as APIs + documentation	AWS launches EC2, S3	Hundreds of adopters
4. Ecosystem Emergence	Others build on you	Third-party value > first-party	Thousands of developers
5. Standard Setting	You define how this is done	AWS APIs become industry standard	Millions of users
6. Meta-Platform	Platforms built on your platform	Heroku on AWS, PlatformIO on Arduino	Entire industries

The essential pattern: Successful platforms evolve through these stages organically, not strategically. You can't skip to Stage 6. You can't design an ecosystem before solving real problems. Platforms emerge from infrastructure, not intention.

Timeline: Typically 5-15 years from Stage 1 to Stage 6. Success requires patience + neutrality + stability.

The Economics of Giving Away the Core

The platform play violates traditional business logic: you give away your core innovation to enable competitors. Arduino open-sourced their hardware designs. ROS gave away its entire codebase. Even AWS published documentation that competitors used to build Azure and Google Cloud.

Why does this work? Because platforms operate on different economics than products:

Traditional Product Logic	Platform Logic
Protect designs with patents	Open-source everything
Maximize profit per unit	Maximize units in ecosystem
Control manufacturing	Enable anyone to manufacture
Own customer relationship	Enable others to serve customers
Capture all value	Create value others can capture

This seems like business suicide, but it creates powerful moats through network effects, switching costs, and ecosystem investment that no product strategy can match.

Case Study: The Shopify Economy

When Shopify realized they couldn't build every feature merchants needed (complex discount rules, loyalty programs, and inventory tools for niche markets), they didn't try to hire more engineers. They turned their product into infrastructure.

By launching the App Store, they invited developers to build and sell features directly to merchants. This creates a powerful flywheel:

1. **Developers** earn revenue by solving niche problems nobody else will solve ("Volume discounts for wholesale pet food in Japan").

2. **Merchants** get features Shopify would never build because the market is too small.

3. **Shopify** gets a sticky ecosystem where merchants can't leave because they rely on five or ten critical plugins.

The plugins lock customers in more tightly than the core product ever could. A merchant using apps for discounts, loyalty, inventory, and shipping has built their entire operational stack on Shopify's platform. Switching means rebuilding everything.

For the developers building these plugins, Shopify represents both opportunity and risk. Many follow the Service Layer Strategy from Chapter 9: a developer consults for a merchant who needs custom discount logic, realizes 500 other merchants need the same thing, and packages it as an App Store plugin. They used paid services to validate the need before building the product.

But developers also face the Platform Dependency risk described later in this chapter. Shopify controls distribution. If a plugin category becomes too popular (basic email marketing, simple discounts), Shopify might build it into the core platform, wiping out plugin businesses overnight. This is the same "Sherlocking" pattern that killed the ChatGPT wrapper startups.

The Shopify economy illustrates the ultimate Platform Play: converting your lack of features into an ecosystem advantage. You don't need to build everything. You need to enable others to build what you can't.

The Trust Problem: Why Platforms Require Long-Term Thinking

Here's the brutal truth about platforms: they require credible commitment to stability. Developers won't invest in learning your platform if they think you'll change APIs next quarter. Companies won't build businesses on your infrastructure if you might shut it down or raise prices.

This is why platforms emerge from patient capital, not venture funding. AWS was funded by Amazon's retail profits. Arduino started as an educational project. ROS was funded by Scott Hassan's Google wealth. Samsung's platform capabilities were built over decades with chaebol patient capital.

The platform play requires thinking in decades, not quarters.

Building ON vs. Building WITH Platforms: The Dependency Decision

The rise of powerful platforms, AWS, OpenAI, Stripe, Shopify, and app stores has created a new innovation paradox. Platforms lower barriers to entry (anyone can launch in days), but they also create existential dependencies. Build on someone else's platform, and you're betting their interests remain aligned with yours. That bet often fails catastrophically.

The pattern is predictable: a platform opens APIs, attracts an ecosystem, then either competes directly with its most successful members or changes terms that make their businesses unviable.

The Platform Dependency Spectrum

Level	Type	Examples	Risk Level
1	Infrastructure Platforms	AWS compute, Stripe payments, Twilio	**Lowest,** you're not competing with their core business
2	Capability Platforms	OpenAI API, Google Maps, SendGrid	**Moderate,** Risk emerges if you reveal valuable use cases
3	Distribution Platforms	iOS App Store, Google Play, Amazon Marketplace	**High,** they control customer access and can change rules arbitrarily
4	Competitive Platforms	Salesforce AppExchange, Facebook Platform, Twitter API	**Existential,** they view ecosystem developers as temporary solutions

The ChatGPT Wrapper Massacre: A Case Study

The launch of the ChatGPT API in early 2023 sparked a gold rush. Hundreds of startups built interfaces to OpenAI's models, PDF chat tools, writing assistants, coding helpers, and research tools. They validated real user needs, acquired paying customers, and raised venture capital. Then OpenAI began rolling out features that made entire categories of wrappers obsolete overnight.

What died:

- "Chat with PDF" startups, OpenAI added native PDF support
- Basic writing assistants, ChatGPT's interface has improved
- Simple coding assistants, GitHub Copilot (OpenAI partnership), expanded
- Research tools, ChatGPT added web search and browsing

These weren't bad products. They were correct interpretations of user needs. But they had zero defensibility. The only moat was being first to wrap OpenAI's API. When OpenAI closed that gap, the moat evaporated.

The brutal lesson: If your entire value proposition is "OpenAI's model + a better interface," you're not building a company, you're conducting unpaid market research for OpenAI.

The Dependency Assessment Framework

Before building on any platform, answer these five questions:

Test	Question	✓ Defensible	✗ Vulnerable
Strategic Alignment	Is your success beneficial to the platform's business model?	SaaS consuming AWS infrastructure	Social feature Facebook might want
Substitutability	Could the platform build your product in a sprint?	Healthcare compliance (AWS has no expertise)	Prettier ChatGPT interface
Data Moat	Are you creating proprietary data/ relationships?	Vertical SaaS owning customer relationships	Aggregating public data via API
Exit Scenario	Can you survive if platform disappears or competes?	Multi-cloud architecture	iOS-only app with no web alternative
Margin Sustainability	Do platform fees leave enough margin?	70% margins after fees	15% margins with 30% platform cut

Platform Dependency Decision Matrix

Situation	Decision
Platform provides commodity infrastructure, your value comes from domain expertise, you own customer relationships	**Build ON platform,** Low risk
Platform fees leave sustainable margins, you have multi-platform options	**Build ON platform,** Manageable risk
Platform is entering your category or acquiring competitors	**Avoid or mitigate, Build abstraction layers**
Your entire value is better UX on their capability	**Avoid,** They'll close the gap
Platform controls distribution and changes rules frequently	**Mitigate heavily,** Multi-platform required
No alternative if platform changes terms	**Critical risk,** Build exit options immediately

The DeepSeek Exception: When Dependency Forces Breakthrough

Ironically, platform dependency sometimes forces breakthrough innovation. DeepSeek's lack of access to NVIDIA H100 chips (Chapter 8) forced algorithmic innovations that reduced reliance on the hardware advantages Western labs took for granted. Being locked out of the platform forced them to build alternatives.

This is the constraint-as-feature pattern applied to platform dependency: when you can't rely on the platform, you build capabilities the platform can't commoditize.

If you're building on platforms by choice, don't expect constraints to save you. Build defensibility deliberately, or accept that you're renting, not building.

Infrastructure as Destiny

The platform play represents the ultimate engineer's leverage. Instead of building solutions, you build the capability for others to build solutions. Instead of solving problems, you enable problem-solving. Instead of competing on features, you compete on ecosystems.

But here's what's crucial: platforms can't be designed top-down. They emerge from solving real problems with infrastructure that others can build upon. AWS emerged from Amazon's internal needs. Arduino emerged from educational constraints. Alibaba emerged from China's trust deficit. Samsung's platform emerged from decades of capability building.

This is why engineers have an advantage in platform building; we build infrastructure naturally. While MBAs see infrastructure as a cost to minimize, engineers see infrastructure as a capability to maximize. We abstract, generalize, and systematize not because we're trying to build platforms but because that's how we think.

You don't need permission to build a platform. You don't need a business model. You don't need to know what others will build. You just need to solve a problem in a way that enables others to solve theirs.

Products have customers. Platforms have ecosystems. Build accordingly.

But platforms require patience, sometimes decades of systematic development before ecosystem effects emerge. Understanding when to persist versus when to pivot requires a framework for the long game: the Technology Readiness Pipeline.

References

1. Zeng, M. (2018). "Alibaba and the Future of Business." Harvard Business Review, September–October 2018.
2. Chang, S. J. (2008). Sony vs Samsung: The Inside Story of the Electronics Giants' Battle for Global Supremacy. John Wiley & Sons.

CHAPTER 11

THE TECHNOLOGY READINESS PIPELINE

For decades, NASA represented the only way to build rockets: spend 20 years in design, test everything on paper, build one perfect system, and pray it works on launch day. The Space Launch System, started in 2011, flew once in 2022 after $23 billion in development. This waterfall approach seemed like the only responsible way to build things that can't fail.

Then SpaceX started blowing up rockets on purpose.

Between 2019 and 2023, SpaceX destroyed dozens of Starship prototypes. SN1 through SN6 burst during pressure tests. SN8, SN9, and SN11 exploded during landing attempts; SN10 touched down successfully before exploding minutes later from a propellant leak. Each explosion was celebrated, not hidden. Each failure taught them something that simulations never could. The aerospace establishment was horrified. The internet was mesmerized. And SpaceX learned faster than any space program in history.

What struck me as profound: SpaceX didn't abandon systematic development; they accelerated it. They weren't building toy rockets or pivoting to different products. They were compressing

NASA's Technology Readiness Levels from decades to months, using real hardware instead of paper studies.

The Technology Readiness Pipeline (TRP) synthesizes these approaches, one framework among many possibilities that combines the rigor of NASA's levels with the speed of SpaceX's iteration. Unlike the Lean Canvas that assumes you're iterating toward product-market fit, the TRP assumes you're building something genuinely new. Unlike the MVP methodology, which creates throwaway prototypes, the TRP ensures each stage contributes to the final system.

Important: This is not a prescription, but an example. The TRP represents patterns I've observed across successful Deep Tech innovations. Some companies follow this sequence naturally. Others forge completely different paths. What matters isn't following these stages religiously; it's understanding the principle that breakthrough innovation requires systematic progression through technical validation before market validation.

The Innovation Portfolio Balance

Before examining the TRP framework in detail, it's crucial to understand where it fits within your overall innovation strategy. Research by Bansi Nagji and Geoff Tuff, published in Harvard Business Review, provides essential context through their innovation portfolio framework.

Successful companies don't choose between methodologies; they balance multiple approaches simultaneously:

Innovation Type	% Portfolio	Primary Methodology	Risk Type	Timeline	Example
Core (Incremental)	70%	Lean Startup, A/B Testing	Market risk	Months	Google search tweaks
Adjacent	20%	Design Thinking	Market + Execution	1-2 years	Gmail for Google users
Transformational	10%	Technology Readiness Pipeline	Technical + Market	5-20 years	Quantum computing

The 70%: Core Innovation

Optimizing existing products for existing customers. Here, Lean Startup excels; you know the market exists, and you're validating specific features or improvements. Fast iteration, A/B testing, and customer feedback loops work brilliantly because customers can articulate their needs.

The 20%: Adjacent Innovation

Expanding into related markets or creating variations of existing products. Design Thinking and customer research help discover latent needs. The technology often works, but you're discovering new applications or user experiences.

The 10%: Transformational Innovation

Creating entirely new categories through technical breakthroughs. This is where TRP applies. The primary uncertainty is whether the technology can work at all, not whether customers want it.

Customer feedback is premature until you cross the Complete Product Threshold.

💡 KEY INSIGHT: *Companies need all three innovation types. Google optimizes search daily (70%), expands into adjacent products like Gmail and Docs (20%), and pursues moonshots like quantum computing and autonomous vehicles (10%). The failure mode isn't choosing the wrong innovation type; it's applying the wrong methodology to your innovation type.*

TRP is designed for the 10%, not the 100%. If you try to run your entire company on TRP timelines, you'll starve before breakthrough arrives. The 70% core innovation funds the 10% transformational bets.

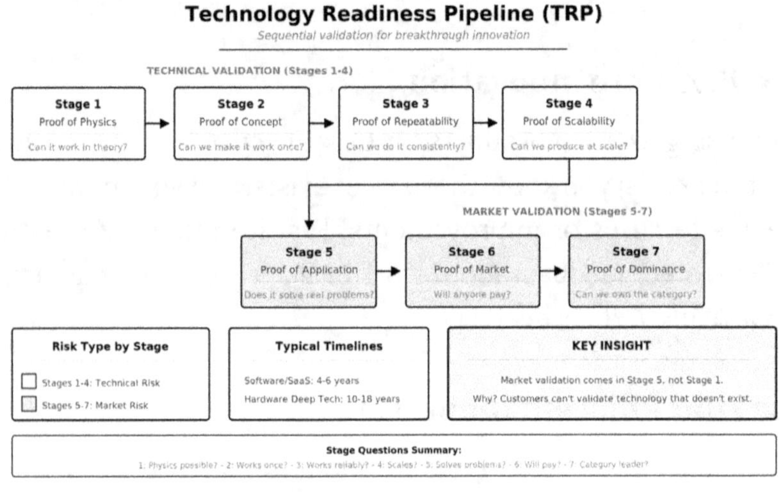

The Seven Stages of the Technology Readiness Pipeline

Stage 1: Proof of Physics

Question: Can this work according to natural laws?
Output: Mathematical models, simulations, basic research
Example: Proving that carbon nanotubes could theoretically be stronger than steel

This is where you explore what physics allows, not what markets demand. The laser researchers proved that stimulated emission could amplify light. The Bitcoin creators proved that distributed consensus was mathematically possible. No customer validation needed or possible.

Stage 2: Proof of Concept

Question: Can we make it work once under controlled conditions?
Output: Laboratory demonstration, proof-of-concept prototype
Example: The first transistor at Bell Labs, working but impractical

Here you move from theory to reality. The prototype doesn't need to be practical, reliable, or economical. It just needs to prove that physics works in practice.

Stage 3: Proof of Repeatability

Question: Can we make it work reliably?
Output: Refined prototype that works consistently
Example: SpaceX landing their first rocket successfully after multiple failures

This stage kills most breakthrough innovations. Making something work once is science. Making it work every time is engineering. This is where you discover the hundred hidden problems that theory didn't predict.

Stage 4: Proof of Scalability

Question: Can we manufacture this efficiently?
Output: Production-ready design, manufacturing process
Example: Tesla is figuring out how to mass-produce battery packs

Now you face the brutal realities of production. Can you source materials? Can you maintain quality at scale? Can you hit cost targets? This is where many innovations die, not because customers don't want them, but because physics makes them too expensive.

Stage 5: Proof of Application

Question: What problems does this actually solve?
Output: Validated use cases, application development
Example: Discovering that lasers could cut, weld, measure, transmit, and heal

Only now, after you know it works, works reliably, and can be manufactured, do you explore applications. This inverts conventional lean methodology, but it's the only sequence that makes sense for breakthrough innovation. The best applications are rarely the first ones discovered.

Stage 6: Proof of Market

Question: Will anyone pay for this?
Output: Business model, pricing validation, early customers
Example: Companies paying millions for the first computers

Finally, market validation appears. But notice: you're not validating whether to build it (it's already built), but how to sell it. This is where traditional innovation methods finally become useful, but only after the technology exists.

Stage 7: Proof of Dominance

Question: Can we own this category?
Output: Market leadership, ecosystem control, standard setting
Example: Google dominating search, ARM defining mobile processors

The final stage is establishing dominance through patents, network effects, ecosystem control, or becoming the de facto standard.

Should You Use TRP? A Self-Assessment

Before diving deeper, establish whether TRP fits your innovation. Answer these questions:

Question	TRP Likely	Lean/Design Thinking Likely
Is your primary uncertainty technical or market-based?	Technical (can it work?)	Market (will they want it?)
Can customers evaluate before it's complete?	No, they need working tech	Yes, mockups suffice
What are iteration costs?	$100K+ and 6+ months	<$10K and <1 month
What are you innovating?	New physics/capabilities	New applications/business models
What's your competitive context?	Creating new category	Competing in existing market

Scoring: If 4-5 answers favor TRP, this framework will serve you well. If 2-3 favor TRP, expect to adapt significantly. If you favor TRP 0-1, consider Lean Startup or Design Thinking instead.

💡 KEY INSIGHT: *TRP works brilliantly for Deep Tech hardware, biotech, and fundamental research where technical validation must precede market validation. It works poorly for software products with known technology, business model innovations, or markets where speed trumps thoroughness.*

Why Market Validation Comes Fifth, Not First

The fundamental heresy of the Technology Readiness Pipeline is that market validation comes in the middle, not at the beginning. This seems to violate everything we're taught about innovation. "Build things people want," Y Combinator preaches. "Get out of the building," Steve Blank insists.

But here's what's crucial: you can't validate demand for something that doesn't exist yet. Customers couldn't validate the need for lasers, transistors, or the internet because these technologies created new categories of possibility. The question isn't "Do customers want this?" but "What becomes possible when this exists?"

The TRP recognizes that breakthrough innovation follows a different sequence:

1. Proof of Physics: Can it work theoretically?
2. Proof of Concept: Can we make it work once?
3. Proof of Repeatability: Can we make it work consistently?
4. Proof of Scalability: Can we make many?
5. **Proof of Application: What problems does it solve?**
6. **Proof of Market: Will anyone pay?**
7. Proof of Dominance: Can we own the category?

Notice that market validation comes sixth, not first. This isn't stubbornness; it's recognition that breakthrough innovations create their own markets.

Skateboard MVP vs. Engineering MVP

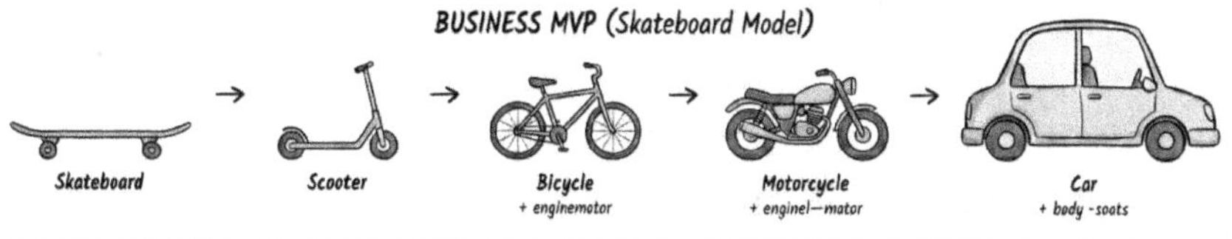

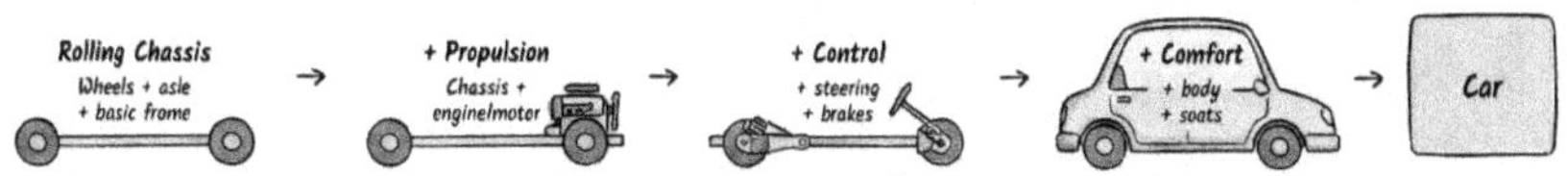

Benefit: Every component in step I exists in final product. Zero production waste (if building the right thing). Learn to build cars by building cars.

Key Differences

Skateboard Model		Engineering Model
Market risk > Technical risk	When to Use	Technical risk > Market risk
Fast iteration is cheap	Risk	Strategic waste if market is wrong
Problem is uncertain	Insurance	Technical foundation is solid

Skateboard works for discovering WHAT to build. Engineering works for discovering HOW to build.

Henrik Kniberg's famous skateboard-to-car illustration, originally designed to show how Agile teams can deliver value incrementally, has become the Lean Startup's visual anthem. But engineers see something troubling in this image.

The progression violates everything we know about system design. It is not iteration; it is repeated, starting over. You learn nothing about *building a car* from building a skateboard. But that is not the skateboard's purpose. Its purpose is to discover whether anyone wants transportation at all.

The Business MVP (Skateboard Model):

- Build a skateboard (tests the transportation hypothesis)
- Throw it away, build a scooter
- Throw it away, build a bicycle
- Throw it away, build a car
- **Production waste**: 3 complete products
- **Information gain:** High

The Engineering MVP (Evolutionary Model):

- Build a rolling chassis (wheels, axle, basic frame)
- Add propulsion (engine or motor)
- Add control systems (steering, brakes)
- Add comfort features (body, seats)
- Refine and optimize
- **Production waste: Zero, assuming you are building the right thing.**

The critical qualifier matters. If the market wants a boat, the entire chassis is waste, and you have learned nothing along the way. The Skateboard model trades production waste for strategic insurance. The Engineering model trades strategic risk for production efficiency.

For breakthrough innovation where technical risk dominates, such as rockets, medical devices, and deep tech, the Engineering model makes sense. You cannot customer-develop your way to new physics. But the wise approach sequences both: validate the problem with low-fidelity methods (interviews, landing pages, concierge service) *before* committing to the chassis. Then build the chassis as your validated foundation.

SpaceX proves you can be agile without being wasteful. The Merlin engine that powers the Falcon 9 today is version 1D, evolved through real-world iterations, including Merlin 1A, 1B, and 1C, each building on actual flight experience. No skateboards. No pivots. Just relentless evolution of real hardware.

The Persistence Premium: Why Sticking Around Beats Pivoting

The "fail-fast" philosophy assumes you can quickly test hypotheses and pivot to something better. But breakthrough innovation operates on a different timeline. What looks like luck is usually persistence meeting opportunity.

Moderna: The Decade Nobody Saw

Moderna's COVID vaccine success wasn't about speed. It was about preparing for a decade while everyone called them crazy. Founded in 2010, they burned $2.5 billion for nine years without a single product.

The persistence timeline:

- **2010-2013:** mRNA considered impossible; they refined delivery systems while competitors pivoted
- **2013-2016:** $450 million raised, zero products; CEO admitted "we were six months from bankruptcy multiple times."
- **2016-2019:** Failed trials, executive departures, devastating press exposés
- **January 2020:** Finalized a COVID vaccine sequence in 48 hours using a decade-old platform

The payoff: First vaccine to trials (63 days), 94.5% efficacy, $18 billion in 2021 revenue.

Every year they didn't pivot, they accumulated irreplaceable expertise. When the world needed mRNA vaccines, only Moderna and BioNTech (who'd also persisted since 2008) could deliver.

The persistence paradox: Moderna's story is inspiring, but dozens of biotech companies have burned through similar amounts, persisting on fundamentally flawed approaches. The challenge is distinguishing productive persistence (hard technical problems worth solving) from stubborn commitment to impossible goals. Moderna had sound science validated through stages; they were refining delivery mechanisms, not hoping physics would change. Knowing the difference between Moderna and Theranos requires technical judgment, not just conviction.

YouTube: Persistence Through the Video Winter

YouTube wasn't the first video platform. The 2000–2004 graveyard was massive: Vimeo, Google Video, RealVideo, and dozens nobody remembers.

YouTube launched in 2005 when three conditions aligned: broadband penetration crossed 50% in the US, Flash video made embedding possible, and digital cameras became ubiquitous. Platforms that quit in 2003 were right about video's future, just two years too early. YouTube's "luck" was surviving long enough for conditions to align.

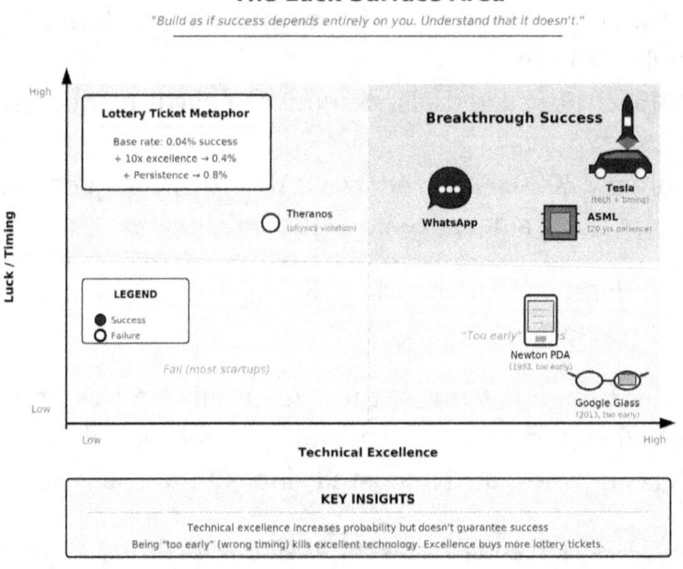

Here's a truth that successful entrepreneurs rarely admit publicly: luck plays a massive role in breakthrough innovation success. Not the only role. But it plays an undeniable role in whether your innovation achieves market success.

Consider the factors outside your control: market timing (is infrastructure ready?), regulatory timing (FDA approval, spectrum allocation), social readiness (privacy norms, cultural acceptance), competitor mistakes, and random events like Moderna's decade of mRNA development becoming essential when COVID arrived.

The "Too Early" Graveyard

Google Glass (2013-2015) exemplifies how excellent technology can fail due to bad timing. The technology worked, but society wasn't ready. A decade later, Meta's smart glasses and Apple's Vision Pro face similar challenges, but social norms have shifted.

Other "too early" innovations: Newton (1993) became iPad (2010). WebTV (1996) became Smart TVs (2010s). QR Codes (1994) took 26 years to find their moment. Being 5 years early is indistinguishable from being wrong.

Technical Excellence Increases Your "Luck Surface Area"

Building excellent technology is like buying lottery tickets. Building mediocre technology is buying one ticket. Building excellent technology is buying a thousand; you still need luck to win, but your odds are dramatically better.

Technical excellence increases your luck surface area because: you survive longer (better technology attracts patient capital), you're ready when opportunity strikes (Moderna spent 10 years building mRNA platforms before COVID arrived), you attract better luck (excellence attracts better engineers and patient investors), and you can survive being early.

As Louis Pasteur observed: "Chance favors the prepared mind." Technical excellence is preparation. Persistence is positioning. Luck is chance. You need all three.

Societal Readiness: The Policy Trap

The European Union's innovation funding has introduced a new dimension to technology assessment: the Societal Readiness Level (SRL). While TRL measures whether technology works, SRL attempts to measure whether society will accept it.

The EU's current SRL pilot is limited to Cluster 5, Climate, Energy, and Mobility, domains where societal acceptance genuinely determines deployment success. For these socially-embedded technologies, considering societal readiness makes sense.

The danger lies in the expansion clause: "possibly widen its use to other fields of application."

If SRL requirements spread to fundamental research funding, the selection mechanism would systematically favor technologies society already understands (incremental), problems already recognized (market-pull), and minimal behavior change required (safe). This is a parallel development fallacy at the policy level.

Consider what would have happened if SRL had been required for historical breakthroughs: mRNA vaccine research in 2010 would have scored SRL 1; society had no framework for understanding messenger RNA therapeutics. CRISPR gene editing would have scored similarly low. Quantum computing remains at SRL 1-2 today.

The Correct Sequence:

- **Stages 1-3 (Physics to Repeatability):** Ignore SRL entirely. Focus on technical feasibility.

- **Stages 4-5 (Scalability to Application):** Begin monitoring SRL. This is reconnaissance, not a gate.
- **Stages 6-7 (Market to Dominance):** Actively invest in improving SRL through demonstration and education.

> 💡 KEY INSIGHT: *Build first, then educate society with what you've built. You cannot conduct meaningful societal dialogue about technologies that don't yet exist.*

If SRL requirements expand from Cluster 5 to fundamental research funding, Europe will systematically select for yesterday's innovations while America and China fund the technologies that will define tomorrow.

When Build First Fails

The graveyard of innovation is filled with technologies that were built before anyone wanted them. Understanding why Build First fails is as important as understanding why it succeeds.

Juicero: Technology Without a Problem

Juicero raised $120 million to build a $700 machine that squeezed proprietary juice packs. The engineering was genuinely impressive, four tons of force, sensors detecting pack freshness, Apple-caliber industrial design.

The problem? Bloomberg reporters discovered you could squeeze the packs by hand and get the same juice. The technology solved a problem that didn't exist. First principles thinking requires identifying actual constraints worth overcoming. Juicero's constraint, "juice packs are hard to squeeze", wasn't real.

Segway: Right Technology, Wrong Integration

Dean Kamen is a legitimate engineering genius. The Segway's self-balancing technology was a genuine breakthrough; the same platform later enabled warehouse robots and mobility aids.

Segway failed because it solved a transportation problem that most people didn't have, at a price point they couldn't justify, in a regulatory environment that didn't accommodate it. The technology worked; the integration insight was missing.

Crucial lesson: Segway's core technology eventually found its applications in warehouses, mobility aids, and last-mile delivery robots. The mistake was assuming that a breakthrough capability automatically implies a breakthrough consumer product.

Google Glass & LLMs: The Institutional Failure Mode

Google Glass represents a different failure mode, one revealing why company context matters as much as technology.

The technology worked. Early adopters in surgery rooms and manufacturing floors found genuine utility. But Google killed it. Why? Google is an advertising company that needs billions of users to matter. A $1,500 device for surgeons wasn't strategic. When public backlash emerged, Google lacked the patience to wait for social acceptance or the focus to pursue the enterprise applications that were working.

The counterfactual: What if Glass had been built by a focused startup? A startup would have noticed that surgery rooms loved Glass and pivoted hard into medical and industrial applications. A startup could have built a sustainable business on tens of thousands of enterprise users while waiting for consumer acceptance to evolve.

Google and LLMs reveal the identical pattern at higher stakes. Google had the transformer architecture ("Attention Is All You Need," 2017), custom TPU chips, and LaMDA, a conversational

AI system sophisticated enough to convince an engineer it was sentient. By any technical measure, Google should have launched ChatGPT.

They didn't. OpenAI did.

Why? Google had too much to lose. Their search advertising business could be cannibalized. Copyright holders were threatening litigation. Every hallucination would be front-page news. OpenAI had none of these constraints, no legacy business, no brand reputation built over decades, and limited legal exposure.

Once the market was validated and the worst barriers absorbed by the pioneer, Google entered. Bard launched within months. Gemini followed. And here's the insight: Google may ultimately win this market. They have what OpenAI doesn't: the full vertical stack. But institutional constraints prevented them from being the pioneers.

The pattern: When Build First happens inside an organization whose success metrics, risk tolerance, or liability exposure don't match the technology's requirements, even superior technology gets delayed or killed.

The Two Risks Framework: Physics Risk vs. Utility Risk

Build First demands first-principles thinking, not just building random cool tech. Understanding why Build First fails requires distinguishing between two fundamentally different risks:

Physics Risk: Can the technology work at all? Does it comply with physical laws? This is what TRP Stages 1-4 address. Theranos failed here; the physics of blood testing made their claims impossible. Dyson succeeded here; cyclonic separation was difficult but physically possible.

Utility Risk: Even if the technology works, does it solve a real problem? Juicero passed the physics test, the engineering was sound, but failed the utility test. The problem it solved wasn't a real constraint.

First principles thinking must validate both: physics feasibility AND problem authenticity.

Build First fails when:

1. The constraint isn't real (Juicero)
2. Integration insight is missing (Segway)
3. Institutional context kills patience (Google Glass, Google LLMs)
4. First principles are wrong (Theranos)

Build First succeeds when:

1. Physics is on your side; the breakthrough is difficult but not impossible
2. The constraint is real; existing solutions are genuinely inadequate
3. You can survive the integration timeline
4. You're positioned to exploit what works

Failure Modes: Recognizing When You're on the Wrong Path

Following any framework dogmatically can be catastrophic. Warning signs that your approach isn't working:

Warning Sign	Question to Ask	Action
Technical validation never converges	Are you encountering expected difficulties or permanent impossibilities?	If physics violation → Quit
Market validation reveals wrong problem	Can your technology solve a different, more valuable problem?	Consider pivot
Running out of runway	Can you raise capital, find consulting revenue, or extend?	SpaceX needed NASA's $1.6B contract
Funded competitors achieving network effects	In winner-take-all markets, is speed more important than thoroughness?	Evaluate acceleration
Personal situation changes	Have you lost energy or passion?	This isn't failure, it's life

The Meta-Failure Mode: Confusing Persistence with Stubbornness

The hardest skill is distinguishing persistence (continuing when fundamentals are sound) from stubbornness (continuing when fundamentals are broken). SpaceX's failed launches showed solvable problems; launch 4 succeeded. Theranos persisted despite physics violations; no amount of persistence would work.

Persist, Pivot, or Quit Decision Framework

Condition	Question	Decision
Problem Value	Is the problem still valuable?	If NO → **QUIT** (wrong problem)
Physics Barrier	Is physics making it impossible?	If YES → **QUIT** (fundamentally impossible)
Technology Fit	Does tech work but solve wrong problem?	If YES → **PIVOT** (apply elsewhere)
Runway	Do you have 12+ months runway?	If YES → **PERSIST** with patience

Red Flags:

- Theranos pattern: Persisting despite physics violations
- Northvolt pattern: Scaling before repeatability proven
- Magic Leap pattern: Marketing before technology works
- Quibi pattern: Perfect execution of a wrong idea

Green Lights:

- SpaceX pattern: Each failure reveals a solvable problem
- Moderna pattern: Sound science, refining delivery
- Tesla pattern: Technology works, iterating to scale

Conclusion: Let Your Innovation Guide Your Methodology

The Technology Readiness Pipeline suggests what many engineers instinctively know: you often can't customer-develop your way to breakthrough innovation. You often can't pivot your way to new physics. You often can't fail-fast when failure costs millions and takes years to recover from.

Notice the word "often." Not "always." Not "never." Often.

That skateboard-to-car illustration isn't how most cars are built. Many innovations follow methodical progression from theoretical possibility through practical reality to market dominance. But not all. YouTube, Moderna, and lasers persisted. Instagram, Slack, and Twitter pivoted. Context matters.

Engineers don't need to apologize for building things "the wrong way" according to any doctrine. The way you naturally think about your specific innovation, systematic or exploratory, sequential or parallel, patient or rapid, is the right way if it matches your innovation's actual structure.

> *The moment you follow a recipe, you're competing*
> *with everyone else following the same recipe.*

No framework is right for everything. The goal isn't finding the one true methodology. It's understanding your innovation deeply enough to know which principles apply and which don't.

Let your innovation guide your methodology. Not vice versa.

But even perfect execution leaves a strategic question unanswered: once you've built your breakthrough, do you compete in an existing market or create a new category entirely? That choice, category creation versus competition, determines whether you fight for market share or transcend competition altogether.

References

1. Orosz, G. (2021). "The Product Development 'Skateboard' Illustration Is Fundamentally Wrong." The Pragmatic Engineer.
2. Nagji, B., & Tuff, G. (2012). "Managing Your Innovation Portfolio." Harvard Business Review, May 2012.
3. Arthur D. Little. (2023). "From Good to Great: Enhancing Innovation Performance." Research Report.
4. Ross, J., & Fonstad, N. (2022). "Forget Fail-Fast: Here's How to Master Digital Innovation." MIT Sloan Management Review, Winter 2022.

CHAPTER 12

CATEGORY CREATION VS. COMPETITION

"Today, Apple is going to reinvent the phone." — Steve Jobs

This distinction, between serving existing markets and creating new categories, represents the fundamental strategic choice in breakthrough innovation. Market-servers ask: "How can we capture share?" Category creators ask: "What game should we be playing?" Market-servers compete. Category creators transcend competition by changing the game itself.

Peter Thiel was right: competition is for losers. The evidence from Apple, Tesla, Amazon Web Services, and others reveals a pattern: category kings don't just win markets, they create and own entire ecosystems. This is the highest form of innovation: not just building better products but defining what "better" means.

The Category King Economics

According to research by Play Bigger (Ramadan, Peterson, Lochhead, & Maney, 2016), category kings capture approximately

76% of the market capitalization in their categories[2]. Not revenue. Market cap. The company that successfully defines and dominates a category takes three-quarters of the total value. Everyone else fights over scraps.

This power law emerges from three reinforcing mechanisms:

Default Thinking: Once markets accept your category definition, you become the default mental model. When people think "search," they think Google. When people think "ride-sharing," they think Uber. Competitors must work against this default, requiring exponentially more effort.

Ecosystem Lock-In: Category kings attract the most developers, partners, and integrations. AWS has millions of certified engineers who think in AWS paradigms. Salesforce has thousands of apps built for its platform. These ecosystems become gravity wells.

Economic Flywheel: Category kings charge premium prices (you're not a commodity), attract the best talent (everyone wants to work for the leader), and access capital cheaply (markets bet on winners). These advantages compound exponentially.

Consider the stark reality of category kings:

Google didn't just win search. It became search. It holds a near-monopoly on market share and commands a valuation that dwarfs all competitors combined.

Meta defined how people spend time on social media and dominated that category for over a decade.

AWS invented cloud computing and continues to capture a

---

2. This finding is based on analysis of ~4,400 U.S. venture-backed technology companies founded since 2000. The researchers identified "category kings" through qualitative scoring of whether firms were creating new market categories. The 76% figure represents an average; individual categories ranged from 70-80%. See Play Bigger's Time to Market Cap report for full methodology.

disproportionate share of industry profits, even as competitors gain ground on market share.

Apple iPhone defined the smartphone category and earns the vast majority of industry profits while selling a fraction of the units. The mathematics explains why creating a new category often beats competing in an existing one. Would you rather be number three in a huge category or number one in a smaller, growing category you defined? The math says create the category.

When to Serve Markets vs. Create Categories

Not every innovation should create a new category. Sometimes serving existing markets with superior execution is the right strategy. The choice depends on multiple factors:

Dimension	Market-Serving	Category Creation
Customer Understanding	Clear needs, established behaviors	Latent needs, new behaviors required
Resources	Limited capital, need quick revenue	Patient capital, can educate market
Timing	Market exists and growing	Technology enables new possibilities
Risk Tolerance	Need predictable returns	Can accept binary outcomes

When Market-Serving Works

Software Incremental Innovation: Facebook's continuous feature improvements, Google's algorithm updates, and most SaaS companies thrive by serving existing markets better. The Lean Startup methodology excels here; rapid iteration, A/B testing, and customer feedback loops all make sense when the market exists, and the question is execution.

Hardware Incremental Innovation: Oura Ring didn't create the wearables category. The Finnish company refined ring-form sensors until they tracked sleep better than existing wristbands. The market existed; they served it with superior technology.

"Sometimes you do have to fight. Where that's true, you should fight and win." — Peter Thiel.

When Category Creation Becomes Necessary

Technology Enables New Possibilities: When breakthroughs make the previously impossible possible, new categories emerge. The laser created multiple categories that couldn't exist before. The internet enabled categories from e-commerce to social media. AI is creating categories we're still discovering.

Existing Categories Are Fundamentally Broken: Uber didn't create a better taxi company; they created a new category of transportation. Netflix didn't create a better video store; they created streaming entertainment. The existing categories were so fundamentally limited that improvement wasn't enough.

Winner-Take-All Dynamics: When network effects or switching costs mean the winner takes everything, creating your own category is often better than competing in someone else's. It's easier to be the king of a new hill than to dethrone an existing king.

The Outcome-Driven Bridge

Between pure market-serving and category creation lies an approach that Tony Ulwick calls Outcome-Driven Innovation. Rather than asking customers what they want (market-serving) or ignoring them entirely (some category creation), you focus on what customers are trying to achieve, their "jobs to be done."

This approach works particularly well when the problem is clear, but solutions aren't, when customers can articulate outcomes but not features, when multiple existing categories partially serve the need, or when technology enables dramatically better outcome achievement.

Consider how this played out with smartphones. The job-to-be-done wasn't "make better phone calls." It was "stay connected and productive anywhere." Once you frame it as outcomes rather than features, the iPhone's radical departure from existing phones makes sense. It wasn't a better phone. It was a better way to achieve the outcome.

Ulwick's research shows that focusing on outcomes rather than customer requests leads to **5x higher success rates** for innovation. It's particularly powerful for engineers because it translates fuzzy customer needs into measurable technical objectives.

Tesla: Category Collision as Strategy

Tesla demonstrates the most sophisticated category creation strategy: forcing two existing categories to collide, creating something new at the intersection.

Traditional automakers saw Tesla as making electric cars, a subcategory of automobiles. But Tesla wasn't making cars that happened to be electric. They were making computers that happened to have wheels. This fundamental category difference explains why traditional automakers still struggle to compete despite superior manufacturing expertise.

"Car as Machine" (Traditional)	"Car as Computer" (Tesla)
Value from mechanical excellence	Value from software capabilities
Annual model year improvements	Continuous over-the-air updates
Dealer service networks	Direct customer relationship
Revenue from sales and maintenance	Revenue from sales, software, and data

When categories collide like this, the company defining the new category usually wins because they're playing a different game. Ford and GM are still trying to build better electric cars. Tesla is building rolling computers. They're not in the same category despite making products that look similar.

Traditional automakers can't pivot to Tesla's category without destroying their existing advantages. Dealer networks become liabilities. Mechanical engineering excellence becomes less relevant. Their entire business model breaks. This is why category collision is so powerful; it doesn't just create competitive advantage, it makes existing advantages worthless.

The Anti-Lean Philosophy of Category Creation

As established in Chapter 1, Lean methodology fails for category creation; customers can't validate categories that don't exist. Peter Thiel's approach aligns: start with secrets (what truth do few agree with?), build monopolies (make competition irrelevant), think in decades (not quarters), and recognize that sales matter as much as product.

None of the category creators, iPhone, Tesla, AWS, SpaceX, followed Lean methodology because they couldn't validate futures others couldn't see.

The UnMarketing of New Categories

When you create a category, traditional marketing fails. You can't position against competitors; there aren't any. You can't emphasize differentiators; the entire category is different. You need what I call *UnMarketing*: education disguised as marketing.

Developer Evangelism vs. Sales

When Amazon launched AWS, they didn't hire enterprise sales reps. They hired developer evangelists, engineers who could teach other engineers. These weren't salespeople who knew technology; they were technologists who could explain and inspire.

AWS's early "marketing" was: technical documentation that taught cloud architecture, white papers explaining distributed systems, certification programs that created AWS-literate engineers, and conferences that were more university than trade show.

By the time competitors emerged, millions of engineers thought in AWS paradigms. The education was the moat.

Movement Building vs. Customer Acquisition

Category creators don't acquire customers; they recruit believers. Tesla owners aren't just customers; they're evangelists for sustainable transport. Apple users aren't just consumers; they're members of a creative class. These companies created movements, not just products.

The playbook for movement building:

1. **Define the enemy:** Gas cars, boring phones, owned software
2. **Paint the future:** Sustainable transport, pocket computers, cloud everything
3. **Create rituals:** Apple keynotes, Tesla reveals, AWS re: Invent

4. **Build community**: User groups, forums, conferences
5. **Reward early believers**: Exclusive access, founder attention, community status

The Category Design Canvas

Based on studying successful category creators, I've developed the Category Design Canvas, a framework for systematically approaching new categories:

1. Point of View (POV)

What's broken about the world that your category fixes?

- Current state problem (what's wrong)
- Future state vision (what's possible)
- The enemy (what must be defeated)
- The stakes (why this matters now)

2. Category Name

What do you call this new thing?

- Different enough to create cognitive distance
- Familiar enough to be understood
- Ownable (you can trademark/defend it)
- Expandable (room for growth)

3. Category Blueprint

What are the rules of this new game?

- Must-have features (table stakes)
- Differentiating capabilities (competitive dimensions)
- Irrelevant factors (what doesn't matter)
- Success metrics (how to keep score)

4. Ecosystem Architecture

Who are the players and what are their roles?

- Your role (platform, enabler, orchestrator)
- Partner roles (developers, integrators, extenders)
- Customer roles (users, buyers, advocates)
- Economic model (who pays whom for what)

5. Education Strategy

How do you teach the market that this category exists?

- Vocabulary (words and concepts)
- Frameworks (mental models)
- Proof points (demonstrations)
- Adoption path (crawl, walk, run)

When Each Method Works: The Meta-Framework

After analyzing hundreds of innovations, clear patterns emerge about when different methodologies succeed:

Innovation Type	Methodology	Key Principle	Examples
Software Incremental	Lean Startup	Low cost, fast feedback	Google A/B tests
Software Breakthrough	Vision + Iteration	Clear vision, flexible execution	iPhone, Gmail
Hardware Breakthrough	Build First, Validate Later	Can't validate what doesn't exist	Tesla, SpaceX
Deep Tech	Technology Readiness Pipeline	Physics before markets	ASML, quantum computing
Biotech/ Pharma	Regulatory First, Market Later	Compliance gates everything	Moderna, BioNTech
Platform	Ecosystem Design	Value from network effects	AWS, Android, Ethereum
Category Creation	Vision + Education	Must teach before selling	Uber, Airbnb, Bitcoin

The crucial insight: Methodology must match context. Using Lean Startup for Deep Tech is like using a hammer on screws, a wrong tool, a wrong result. Using heavy R&D processes for software iteration is overkill that slows you down.

The Danger of Category Creation Recipes

Here's the paradox that must be acknowledged: the moment category creation becomes a recipe, it fails. The Play Bigger consultancy has turned category design into a structured methodology with certifications. But following their recipe means you're doing what others are doing, which by definition isn't category creation.

True category creation requires what Thiel calls *thinking for yourself*. It requires seeing what others don't see, building what others won't build, and persisting when others quit. There's no template for this. There's no canvas that guarantees success. Category creation is an act of will and vision, not process and methodology.

The frameworks I've shared, the Category Design Canvas and the Innovation Context Matrix, aren't recipes. They're tools for thinking, not templates for execution. Use them to clarify your thinking, not to replace it.

Conclusion: Competition Is for Losers

When you compete in existing markets, you accept the game as defined. You fight for a share in someone else's category. Even if you win, you've won a game someone else created.

Category creators don't compete; they transcend competition by changing the game. They don't capture market share; they create markets. They don't fight for customers; they educate believers. They don't optimize for existing metrics; they define new ones.

For engineers, this is liberating. You don't need to be better at business than MBAs. You don't need to out-market marketers. You need to build something so fundamentally different that existing rules don't apply. Your technical insight becomes the foundation for new categories that business-minded competitors can't imagine.

The choice is yours: compete in existing categories with incremental improvements, or create new categories with breakthrough innovations. The first path is safer, more predictable, and easier to teach. The second path is harder, riskier, but ultimately more rewarding.

Categories aren't discovered. They're created by someone.

Why not you?

But in the age of AI, category creation faces a new challenge: when everyone can build anything, how do you create something that can't be instantly replicated? That is the AI Paradox, and we must confront it next.

References

1. Thiel, P., & Masters, B. (2014). Zero to One: Notes on Startups, or How to Build the Future. Crown Business.
2. Ramadan, A., Peterson, D., Lochhead, C., & Maney, K. (2016). Play Bigger: How Pirates, Dreamers, and Innovators Create and Dominate Markets. Harper Business.
3. Ulwick, A. (2016). Jobs to be Done: Theory to Practice. Idea Bite Press.
4. Christensen, C. M. (1997). The Innovator's Dilemma: When New Technologies Cause Great Firms to Fail. Harvard Business Review Press.
5. Isaacson, W. (2011). Steve Jobs. Simon & Schuster.
6. Felin, T., Gambardella, A., Stern, S., & Zenger, T. (2019). "Lean Startup and the Business Model: Experimentation Revisited." Long Range Planning, 53(4).

CHAPTER 13

THE AI PARADOX

Rich Sutton, one of the pioneers of reinforcement learning, published an influential essay in 2019 called "The Bitter Lesson." His core argument: general methods that leverage computation ultimately outperform hand-crafted domain knowledge. Deep Blue beat Kasparov through brute-force search. AlphaGo beat Lee Sedol through scale and self-play. Current foundation models beat benchmarks through massive data and computing.

The lesson has been embraced by AI labs and corporate strategists alike. Scale solves everything. More compute, more data, more progress.

They're half right.

Yes, scaling works for AI research. But not for the reasons the establishment thinks. And it won't create innovation the way they imagine.

Here's the paradox: The Bitter Lesson is about building AI systems, not about innovation itself. The lesson says computation beats hand-crafted rules for AI tasks. It doesn't say AI will innovate for you. Confusing tool-building progress with innovation progress will waste the next decade of corporate strategy.

The establishment sees AI generating millions of molecular

structures and declares innovation will be "accelerated." But they're measuring *invention* (creating new things), not *innovation* (creating new value through real-world implementation).

Use AI, But Don't Be Used By It

Let me be crystal clear: You should absolutely use AI. Every tool that amplifies human capability should be embraced. I use AI daily. My engineer friends use AI constantly.

Even if AI could propose every possible system, someone must still decide which one is worth building. Generation is not selection. Invention is not innovation.

But here's what separates builders from talkers: We use AI to eliminate routine work, not to eliminate thinking. We use it to accelerate execution, not to replace vision. We use it to test more hypotheses, not to avoid forming hypotheses.

The trap isn't using AI. The trap is believing AI will innovate for you.

The establishment falls directly into this trap. They confuse AI's ability to generate options with the human ability to recognize which option matters. They mistake computational power for creative power. They conflate pattern matching with pattern breaking.

The Invention-Innovation Confusion

Look closely at what AI labs are actually celebrating:

What AI Did	What Innovation Requires
AI predicted 200 million protein structures	Finding the ONE that works in humans might take 10-15 years
Generated millions of drug candidates	$2.6 billion per approved drug, 90% failure rate
Created dozens of store configurations	Understanding which layout drives customer behavior
Designed rocket engines with novel geometries	System integration that makes engines actually fly

All *invention*. Zero *innovation*.

Think of it through the Luck Surface Area framework. AI lets you buy millions of lottery tickets (generate candidates). But it doesn't help you hold the winning ticket (find the one that actually works). Invention is buying tickets. Innovation is winning.

Innovation isn't generating 200 million protein structures. It's finding the ONE that actually works in a human body, navigating FDA approval, scaling manufacturing, and getting it to patients. That takes 10-15 years and $2.6 billion per approved drug.

R&D productivity is declining. Eroom's Law (Moore's Law reversed) shows drug discovery costs doubling every nine years. Good ideas are harder to find. Yet we celebrate AI generating millions of new ideas.

The contradiction is glaring. The problem was never finding ideas. The pharmaceutical industry already tests millions of compounds. The constraint isn't generating candidates.

Economists call this the Jevons Paradox applied to innovation: as the cost of generating ideas drops to zero, the demand for *filtering* those ideas skyrockets. We are drowning in options, not solutions.

To be fair, AI helps with real constraints: computational biology predicts toxicity earlier, automation reduces testing costs, and better trial design accelerates timelines. AI might cut drug development costs in half and shave years off development. That's significant.

But core innovation challenges remain human: deciding which diseases are worth targeting, understanding complex biological systems holistically, navigating regulatory landscapes, building relationships with health systems, and persisting through decades of uncertainty.

AI helps with the $2.6 billion problem. It doesn't help with the "which molecule actually matters" problem. That's the difference between *invention* (generating options) and *innovation* (creating value).

The Ladder of Causation

Judea Pearl, who won the Turing Award for his work on causal reasoning, provides a framework that explains why AI struggles with innovation. In "The Book of Why," he describes three levels of cognitive ability:

Rung 1: Association.

What is? Finding correlations and making predictions based on observed data.

Rung 2: Intervention.

What if I do? Understanding causal effects of actions.

Rung 3: Counterfactuals.

What if I had done differently? Imagining worlds that don't exist.

Current AI systems, including the latest foundation models and multimodal architectures, operate almost entirely on Rung 1. They find patterns in existing data. As Pearl puts it: "All the impressive achievements of deep learning amount to just curve fitting."

Innovation requires Rung 3. You have to imagine products that don't exist, markets that haven't formed, and solutions to problems people don't know they have. AI can find patterns in what exists. It cannot imagine what should exist.

The Low-Hanging Fruit Trap

Here's what most executives don't understand: The AI revolution is creating a massive trap, the systematic pursuit of low-hanging fruit that looks like innovation but isn't.

Look at what analysts celebrate as "AI innovation wins": supply chain optimization that saves 2% on logistics, chatbots that handle customer service tickets faster, A/B testing that improves conversion rates by 0.3%, and predictive maintenance that reduces downtime by 15%.

These are efficiency gains. Operational improvements. Doing the same things slightly better. **But they're not innovation, they're optimization.**

The danger isn't that these improvements are worthless. The danger is that companies will exhaust their innovation capacity chasing easy wins while competitors who aim for the stars will eventually dominate.

The Commodity Trap

When everyone has access to the same AI tools, what differentiates you? Not your ability to generate ideas, AI does that. Not your ability to optimize existing products, AI does that better. Not your ability to follow "best practices", those are literally encoded in AI's training data.

Every competitor can generate the same product ideas. Every startup can build the same MVP. Every company can run the same optimizations. The entire Lean Startup methodology can now be automated. The innovation theater from Chapter 1 has been turbocharged into an epidemic of trend-following.

The AI Medical Scribe Explosion (2024-2025)

In early 2024, the AI medical scribe market was nascent. By late 2025, over a dozen serious competitors emerged, building virtually identical products: Nuance DAX Copilot, Ambience Healthcare, Freed, Suki AI, Abridge, DeepScribe, and dozens more.

Every startup followed the same playbook:

1. Validate the pain point (doctors hate documentation)
2. Build MVP with accessible AI tools (open-source transcription + frontier language models)
3. Iterate based on customer feedback (add EHR integration)
4. Race to market before competitors

The outcome? When Epic (the EHR giant) launched its native AI scribe in September 2025, many of these startups faced existential threats overnight.

This is the "Sherlocking" pattern from Chapter 10 in action. These startups were building at Level 2 (Capability Platforms) with AI APIs and Level 3 (Distribution Platforms) with EHR systems. The Platform Dependency Decision Matrix warned: "If your entire value is better UX on their capability, they'll close the gap." Epic closed the gap.

Similar patterns emerged in computer vision sports tracking, AI writing assistants, and the infamous "wrapper graveyard", startups that were simply interfaces to foundation model APIs, wiped out by a single feature update from their technology provider.

The brutal truth: These founders aren't wrong to validate customer needs or use accessible AI tools. They're wrong to think this leads to sustainable competitive advantage. When everyone has access to the same models and the same iteration frameworks, the only differentiation becomes who executes slightly better or who got funding to subsidize customer acquisition.

That's not innovation. That's a race to commoditization.

The Restaurant-ification of Tech

Peter Thiel famously warned that competitive markets destroy profits, citing restaurants as the prime example: industries where barriers to entry are low, differentiation is minimal, and margins are razor-thin.

AI has just turned software into the restaurant business.

When AI coding assistants can generate code in seconds, the technical barrier that used to protect startups has collapsed. Your six-month head start on an incremental feature is now a six-day head start for a competitor.

The parallel is exact: Low barriers to entry. Minimal differentiation. Razor-thin margins. Most fail. In restaurants, the difficulty isn't cooking. In AI-era software, the difficulty isn't coding. Both require finding a sustainable competitive advantage when everyone has the same basic capabilities.

If you are building something that can be built by a competitor with AI tools in a weekend, you are not building a company. You are exploiting a temporary market inefficiency that is about to be arbitraged away.

This makes the "Build First" philosophy existential. The only sustainable advantages left are the ones AI cannot commoditize:

Proprietary data AI can't access (your unique customer data, workflows, insights)

Network effects that lock in users before competitors arrive

Regulatory moats (AI can't navigate healthcare compliance, financial regulations)

Physical world integration (hardware, supply chains, manufacturing)

Zero-to-one breakthroughs that create entirely new categories

AI makes incremental innovation trivial. **This makes breakthrough innovation the only innovation that matters.**

When anyone can build a restaurant, you need to invent fast food. When anyone can clone software, you need to build AWS.

Why AI Can't Innovate (Only Invent)

AI Excels At	Innovation Requires
Successful past examples	Breaking from successful patterns
Statistical correlations	Understanding causation
Average of training data	Extreme outliers that change everything
Interpolation between known points	Extrapolation beyond all boundaries

Gary Marcus, the cognitive scientist who founded Geometric Intelligence (later acquired by Uber), has documented these limitations for decades. His core insight: neural networks can interpolate within their training distribution but fail to extrapolate beyond it. In 1998, he showed that networks trained on even numbers couldn't generalize to odd numbers. In 2024, Apple researchers demonstrated that the same limitation persists in today's most advanced models.

Current AI architectures learn from successful patterns in their training data. They perfected "faster horses." They can't conceive automobiles.

The Agentic AI Exception (That Proves the Rule)

The latest AI trend, "agentic AI," promises systems that autonomously plan, act, and use tools. These systems move beyond generating text to executing multi-step tasks: booking travel, analyzing code repositories, conducting market research, and managing supply chains.

This seems to address the "AI can't innovate" critique. If AI can autonomously plan and execute, hasn't it crossed the threshold into genuine innovation capability?

The answer reveals why autonomy and innovation remain fundamentally different.

Agentic AI operates brilliantly within known solution spaces. Give it a goal like "optimize warehouse layout" or "debug this codebase," and it can plan steps, use tools, iterate on failures, and reach solutions humans would take weeks to achieve. But notice what these tasks have in common: the solution space is defined, the success criteria are measurable, and the paths to success exist in training data.

These are *closed-world problems*: the rules are known, success is measurable, and the solution space is bounded. Innovation happens in *open-world domains* where the rules haven't been written, success criteria don't yet exist, and the problem space is unbounded.

Rodney Brooks, who co-founded iRobot and ran MIT's AI Lab for a decade, puts it bluntly: "Someone suggested to me recently that it would be cool and efficient to tell his warehouse robots where to go by building an LLM for his system. In his estimation, however, this is not a reasonable use case... it would actually slow things down."

Think of it this way: An agent is the ultimate "skateboard" builder. It can convert a skateboard into a scooter, and a scooter into a bicycle. But it cannot look at a bicycle and conceptualize a car. That leap requires disconnecting from the training data, imagining a fundamentally different paradigm. Agents optimize within paradigms. They don't create new ones.

The distinction: Agentic AI automates execution within existing paradigms. Innovation creates new paradigms. This makes agentic AI extraordinarily valuable for the 70% incremental optimization and useful for the 20% adjacent innovation. But it remains fundamentally unable to create the 10% breakthrough innovation that redefines what's possible.

The Long Tail of Failure

Brooks offers another insight that explains why AI struggles in the real world:

> *"Without carefully boxing in how an AI system is deployed, there is always a long tail of special cases that take decades to discover and fix. Paradoxically, all those fixes are AI-complete themselves."*

Tesla's Full Self-Driving illustrates this perfectly. After more than a decade of development, billions of dollars invested, and millions of vehicles generating training data, the system still requires constant human supervision. It struggles with railroad crossings, construction zones, and unusual lane markings. Light rain can disable the system entirely.

Tesla's own instructions to users: "It may do the wrong thing at the worst time, so you must always keep your hands on the wheel."

The lesson isn't that Tesla engineers are incompetent. The lesson is that the real world has an infinite supply of edge cases, and AI systems that work brilliantly 99% of the time can fail catastrophically in the remaining 1%. That 1% is where innovation lives: the unexpected situations, the problems no one anticipated, the opportunities hiding in complexity.

If AI can't reliably handle a railroad crossing after years of trying, how will it imagine entirely new product categories?

The long-tail problem points to a deeper limitation: AI generates components, not systems.

The Integration Challenge

Remember Chapter 8 on systems thinking? AI can generate molecular candidates, but it cannot design, validate, and run clinical trials end-to-end. It can optimize store layouts, but it cannot model the deeper psychological and cultural forces that drive human behavior. It can assist in generating rocket engine components, but it cannot perform the systems integration required to make an actual engine fly.

Yejin Choi, the MacArthur Fellow who leads commonsense AI research at the University of Washington and Allen Institute, explains the gap: "AI doesn't understand the world. It understands the text about the world. Big difference."

AI doesn't understand emergent properties, how components

interact to create something greater than their sum. It can't grasp feedback loops that only appear at scale. It doesn't recognize when a constraint in one area creates an opportunity in another.

AI doesn't understand *why* constraints matter (Chapter 9). To AI, a chip embargo is just missing data, not an opportunity for algorithmic innovation. AI can't distinguish between human rules and physical laws (Chapter 4). It treats "that's how we've always done it" the same as "thermodynamics prevents this."

The Incumbency Amplifier

Here's a sobering reality: Big incumbents may actually slow innovation by using AI to entrench their positions.

Large firms use AI not to innovate, but to optimize existing monopolies: making search incrementally better rather than reimagining information discovery, optimizing ad targeting rather than creating new social paradigms, squeezing suppliers harder rather than revolutionizing commerce.

To be fair, these companies also pursue breakthrough innovation through dedicated research labs. But the bulk of their AI investment goes toward defending existing positions rather than creating new categories.

Disruptive innovation often comes from constrained new entrants rather than established players with resources to spare.

The New Innovation Landscape

Be clear about what AI does brilliantly, and use it for exactly these things:

The 70/20/10 Framework

Category	AI Role	Human Role	Strategic Implication
Incremental (70%)	Automate completely	Oversight only	Table stakes - AI makes this a commodity
Adjacent (20%)	Generate options & analyze	Select, combine & judge	The battleground - where strategy matters
Breakthrough (10%)	Minimal - mainly documentation	Vision, persistence & integration	The moat - where legends are built

The 20% adjacent space is critical because it's not commoditized like the 70%, but not as rare as the 10%. This is where knowing how to use AI strategically, not just having access to it, becomes the differentiator.

Examples of winning in the 20%: taking existing technology into new markets (AI analyzes data, humans recognize cultural nuances), combining existing components in novel ways (AI generates combinations, humans recognize emergent value), scaling successful experiments (AI optimizes metrics, humans know when to break the optimization for strategic reasons).

> **KEY INSIGHT:** The real competition isn't in the 70% that AI automates. It's not even in the 10% breakthrough innovation. The battle is in the 20% adjacent space where AI amplifies human judgment rather than replacing it.

What Becomes Scarcer and More Valuable

As AI democratizes invention, five capabilities become priceless:

Vision. AI sees patterns in existing data. Value comes from seeing what should exist but doesn't. Steve Jobs didn't ask AI what phone to build. He saw a future where the phone was everything else.

Taste. AI generates millions of variations. Value comes from knowing which ONE matters. This is the human answer to the Jevons Paradox: when options are infinite, filtering becomes everything.

Persistence. AI optimizes for quick wins. Value comes from 20-year commitments to hard problems. While competitors pivot based on AI-generated insights, you continue building nuclear reactors.

Systems Architecture. AI creates individual components. Value comes from understanding emergent properties, knowing when 1+1=3.

Category Creation. AI optimizes existing categories. Value comes from inventing entirely new games. AWS wasn't a better hosting option; it was a new category. Tesla wasn't a better car; it was a computer on wheels.

The Bootstrap Advantage in the AI Age

The bootstrap mentality (Chapter 7) becomes even more powerful. While VC-funded startups use AI to optimize their burn rate, bootstrapped companies use constraints to force innovation.

Bootstrap constraints force mastery of the 20% adjacent space. Without endless capital to chase every AI-generated possibility, bootstrapped teams must develop the taste to know which AI suggestions to pursue, which to modify, and which to ignore.

The Service Layer Strategy becomes unstoppable when AI handles repetitive analysis, report generation, and code generation, while humans focus on novel problem-solving, deep customer understanding, and judgment calls.

The combination is lethal. AI eliminates the drudgery. Humans provide the insight. Engineers spend zero time on boilerplate code, 100% on solving new problems.

DeepSeek and the Constraint Advantage

DeepSeek offers a striking counter-example to the "more resources = more innovation" thesis.

Faced with US chip embargoes, Chinese researchers couldn't just throw more compute at the problem. They had to innovate differently. The result: performance approaching Western frontier models at a fraction of the training cost. The establishment would have recommended buying more GPUs. The embargo forced algorithmic innovation.

Map this onto the Luck Surface Area framework. DeepSeek started in what looked like the worst position: Low Luck (embargoes blocking access to frontier hardware). But they used constraints to force movement up the Technical Excellence axis. Rather than waiting for luck to change, they increased their technical surface area until breakthroughs became inevitable.

This validates the constraint innovation matrix from Chapter 8: Extreme constraints + clear objectives = breakthrough innovation. One insight from constrained engineering can outperform a million iterations from unconstrained resources.

The Stealth Mode Imperative

Here's a critical strategic shift that most innovators haven't grasped: In the AI age, keeping your breakthrough ideas secret until you have a working product isn't paranoia, it's survival.

Remember the Technology Readiness Pipeline from Chapter 11? In the pre-AI world, you could talk about your idea at Stage 2 or 3 because competitors needed years to catch up. Not anymore.

With AI, the time from idea to implementation has collapsed. A competitor can prototype your concept in days. They can generate 100 variations in hours. They can test market positioning before you've finished building. They can raise funding with AI-generated demos.

The first-mover advantage, already fragile (Chapter 7), becomes nearly worthless when second-movers can replicate and improve your innovation in weeks instead of years.

> **KEY INSIGHT:** Stages 3-4 of the TRP are where you're most vulnerable. You've proven it works, but haven't built defensibility. This is when a competitor with AI tools could replicate years of work in weeks.

The TRP-AI Vulnerability Matrix

Stages 1-4 (Physics through Scalability): Absolute secrecy. No pitch decks. No accelerators. No networking events. Just you and your small team building. AI can't copy what it doesn't know exists.

Stage 5 (Proof of Application): Careful, limited disclosure under strict NDAs. Assume anything you share will be replicated within weeks.

Stage 6 (Proof of Market): Launch with a complete, working product that's already defensible. By the time competitors understand what you've built, you've established technical moats, customer relationships, and operational excellence.

This perfectly aligns with the bootstrap approach. When you're not raising money, you don't need to pitch. When you're funding through revenue, you don't need to explain your vision to VCs who might fund your competitors.

New Rules for Innovation Disclosure

Never share the breakthrough insight. Share the problem being solved, not how it's being solved. If someone asks about the approach, describe the outcome, not the method.

Patents can wait. Filing patents early just teaches competitors the approach. Better to have trade secrets and operational excellence than published patents that competitors can read.

The team is the moat. In the AI age, the only people who should fully understand an innovation are the people building it. Everyone else gets the marketing version.

Launch fully formed. The MVP approach assumes customer feedback is needed to build the right thing. But in breakthrough innovation, the target is already clear. Launch when it's defensible, not when it's viable.

The Pioneer's Paradox

We've entered a strange new era: AI makes it easier than ever to be a pioneer (you can build faster), but harder than ever to maintain a pioneer advantage (others can copy faster).

The solution isn't to move faster; it's to move secretly. Build in the shadows. Perfect in private. Launch when you're unstoppable.

As we explored throughout this book, real innovation doesn't come from pivoting based on feedback or iterating toward product-market fit. It comes from having the conviction to build something genuinely new. In the AI age, that conviction must be paired with the discipline to build it quietly.

And finally, it requires knowing when to emerge from the shadows, when 'later' finally arrives.

References

1. Pearl, J., & Mackenzie, D. (2018). The Book of Why: The New Science of Cause and Effect. Basic Books.
2. Marcus, G. (2018). "Deep Learning: A Critical Appraisal." arXiv:1801.00631.
3. Brooks, R. (2024). "LLMs and Robotics." Rodney Brooks Blog.
4. Choi, Y. (2022). "Commonsense AI: Myth and Truth." Allen Institute for AI.
5. Apple Research. (2024). "GSM-Symbolic: Understanding the Limitations of Mathematical Reasoning in Large Language Models." arXiv.
6. Thiel, P. (2014). Zero to One: Notes on Startups, or How to Build the Future. Crown Business.

CHAPTER 14

MARKET LATER

"The best marketing doesn't feel like marketing." — Tom Fishburne

The previous chapter explained why stealth matters in the AI age. Build in the shadows. Perfect in private. Launch when you're unstoppable. But eventually, "later" arrives. You've built something real. The shadows served their purpose. Now what?

This is the moment the book's title has been pointing toward. You've done the hard work: first-principles thinking, systems design, technical moats, patient development through the Technology Readiness Pipeline. You resisted the pressure to validate prematurely. You ignored the voices telling you to pivot, to ship faster, to get customer feedback before you had something worth showing.

Now comes a different challenge. The skills that made you a great builder are not the skills that will make your innovation succeed in the market. The discipline that kept you focused on physics and engineering must now expand to include perception and communication.

This chapter is about that transition. But transitioning to market requires knowing what kind of market you're entering. Markets exist in three states relative to your innovation:

- **Non-existent market**: No one is buying anything in this category because the category doesn't exist yet. (The laser in 1960)
- **Unarticulated market:** People have the problem but cannot request your solution because they can't imagine it. (Smartphones before iPhone)
- **Ready market**: Customers can articulate needs and evaluate solutions. (Better food delivery apps)

Lean methods work for ready markets. This book is about the other two.

When "Later" Arrives

The timing question haunts every technical founder. Market too early and you burn credibility with a product that isn't ready. Market too late and competitors define the category without you. Both failures are common. Both are avoidable.

The Technology Readiness Pipeline provides clear signals. "Later" typically arrives at TRP Stage 5 (Application Validation) or Stage 6 (Market Entry). Before Stage 5, you're still proving the technology works. Marketing at this point is premature. You're making promises your product can't keep.

But TRP stages are internal metrics. What are the external signals that "later" has arrived?

Repeatability. You can demonstrate your innovation multiple times with consistent results. The first prototype working once is not enough. The tenth demonstration working reliably is the threshold.

Explainability. You can explain the value proposition in terms that non-engineers understand. If you can only describe your innovation in technical specifications, you're not ready to market. The translation to customer value must be complete.

Defensibility. Your technical moat is established. Marketing attracts attention, including from competitors. Before you step into the light, your advantages should be difficult to replicate quickly.

Scalability. You have a credible path to serving demand. Marketing that works creates customers. If you cannot serve those customers, successful marketing becomes a liability.

When all four conditions are met, "later" has arrived. Not before.

The danger for engineers is waiting for perfection. There is always one more feature to add, one more test to run, one more edge case to handle. Engineers call it being thorough. It's perfectionism, and it keeps innovations in the lab forever. The four signals above are sufficient. They do not require perfection. They require readiness.

Market later does not mean market at perfection. It means market at readiness. Readiness is about repeatability, explainability, defensibility, and scalability, not completeness.

When the Breakthrough Is Perceptual

Not all innovation requires new physics. Sometimes the technology exists, but the meaning doesn't.

Rory Sutherland, in his book *Alchemy*, refers to this as the realm of "psychological moonshots." His central observation is that humans are not rational optimizers. We respond to framing, context, and meaning. Sometimes the engineering solution is the wrong tool entirely.

Consider Tesla's "Ludicrous Mode." The underlying technology (instant torque from electric motors) existed in every Tesla. But naming it and making it a selectable mode with a theatrical countdown transformed a specification into an experience. The car doesn't accelerate faster because of the name. But owners *feel* something different when they press that button. A 0-60 time is a number. Ludicrous Mode is a story you tell at dinner parties.

This is perceptual innovation: changing what people believe, not what the product does.

James Dyson understood this intuitively. The clear dustbin on his vacuum cleaner wasn't an engineering necessity. Bagless cyclone technology works fine with an opaque container. The transparency was psychological proof that the machine worked. Consumers could *see* the dirt accumulating. Competitors could copy the cyclone technology. They couldn't copy the theater of visible performance.

We saw this principle earlier with IKEA. The flat-pack constraint forced customers to assemble their own furniture, originally a cost-saving measure. But psychologists later documented the "IKEA effect", people value things more when they've invested effort in creating them. What started as a logistics constraint became a psychological advantage. The bookshelf you assembled yourself *means* more than one that was delivered pre-built.

The danger for engineers is assuming every problem needs an engineering solution. We're trained to optimize measurable performance. But sometimes the gap isn't between your product and the competition. It's between your product and how people *perceive* your product.

This suggests three types of innovation:

Technical breakthrough changes what's physically possible. The laser, mRNA vaccines, and reusable rockets. This requires first-principles thinking, deep technical moats, and the patience of the Technology Readiness Pipeline. It's what most of this book addresses.

Systems innovation changes how components interact. Toyota's production system, the Internet's protocol stack, and ARM's licensing model. The individual pieces exist; the breakthrough is in their arrangement.

Perceptual innovation changes how humans interpret. Tesla's Ludicrous Mode, Dyson's clear bin, IKEA's assembly pride. No new physics required, just a deeper understanding of psychology than competitors possess.

Most breakthrough innovations combine elements of all three. Tesla's success isn't just battery technology (technical) or vertical integration (systems). It's also the identity of driving electric (perceptual).

If your technology already works and customers still aren't buying, the problem may not be technical. It may be perceptual. The instinct to build a better product might be exactly wrong. Sometimes you need to build a better *understanding* of the product.

The questions shift:

Instead of "How do I make it work better?" ask "How do I make it *feel* better?"

Instead of "What features should I add?" ask "What do customers *believe* about this category?"

Instead of "How do I improve performance?" ask "How do I *demonstrate* performance?"

The engineer who dismisses this as "just marketing" will lose to the engineer who understands that perception is reality for the humans who buy products.

The Engineer's Marketing Toolkit

You don't need to become a marketer. You need to understand what marketers do and identify the parts you should own versus delegate.

What engineers should own:

Technical storytelling. No one can explain what you built better than you. The challenge is translating technical achievement into human value. "Our algorithm reduces latency by 40%" means nothing to customers. "Your video calls won't freeze anymore" means everything. The engineer who built it should craft the core narrative, then let marketers amplify it.

Proof of performance. Demonstrations, benchmarks, technical comparisons. When AWS launched, its "marketing" was largely documentation and tutorials. Engineers trust other engineers. Your ability to show rather than tell is a marketing advantage that professional marketers cannot replicate.

Developer and technical relations. If your customers are technical, your marketing should be too. Developer evangelism, technical blog posts, conference talks, open-source contributions. These are marketing activities that require engineering credibility.

Product decisions that communicate. Dyson's clear dustbin was a product decision with marketing impact. Tesla's over-the-air updates communicate "this car improves over time" without any advertising. The engineering choices you make send messages. Be intentional about what they say.

What engineers should delegate:

Brand development. Visual identity, tone of voice, positioning statements. These require skills most engineers don't have and shouldn't try to develop. Find partners who understand brand building.

Demand generation. Advertising, SEO, paid acquisition, lead nurturing. These are technical disciplines in their own right. Specialists will outperform generalists.

Market research. Understanding customer segments, competitive positioning, and pricing psychology. This is where design thinking and customer research methods (which we critiqued for technical development) actually belong. Once you have something real, learning how customers perceive it is valuable.

The division is simple: own the substance, delegate the style. Own what requires technical credibility, delegate what requires marketing expertise.

From Building to Selling

The transition from building to selling is awkward for most engineers. Building is about truth: does it work or not? Selling feels like persuasion, spin, and manipulation. This discomfort is partly justified and partly misguided.

It's justified because bad marketing *is* manipulative. Overpromising, hiding limitations, creating artificial urgency. Engineers are right to distrust these tactics. They violate the engineering ethic of honest assessment.

It's misguided because good marketing is translation, not manipulation. You've built something valuable. Customers need to understand that value. Failing to communicate clearly isn't integrity; it's negligence. If your innovation could help people, but they never learn about it, you've failed them.

Peter Thiel makes this point directly in *Zero to One*: engineers underestimate sales because they underestimate how hard it is. Great salespeople make selling look effortless, which makes engineers think it requires no skill. The opposite is true. Sales and marketing are disciplines with their own rigor.

The transition requires a mindset shift:

From "the product should speak for itself" to "the product needs a voice."

From "features" to "benefits."

From "what we built" to "what you can do."

From "technical accuracy" to "emotional resonance."

None of this requires abandoning truth. It requires expanding your definition of what matters. Technical specifications are true. Customer outcomes are also true. Both deserve articulation.

The Marketing Anti-Patterns

Engineers entering marketing for the first time make predictable mistakes. Recognizing them helps you avoid them.

Marketing before the product works. This is the Lean Startup failure mode applied to marketing. You launch campaigns for a product that isn't ready, get customers, disappoint them, and destroy trust. Marketing amplifies whatever exists. If the product is broken, marketing amplifies the brokenness. This is especially dangerous in the AI age. AI makes it trivial to demonstrate capability. It does not make it trivial to deploy reliability. Marketing the demo creates expectations that the system cannot meet. Demos impress. Systems deliver.

Over-engineering the message. Engineers love precision. Marketing requires simplification. The message "Our proprietary algorithm uses transformer architecture with custom attention mechanisms to achieve state-of-the-art performance on standard benchmarks" is precise and useless. "It works twice as fast" is imprecise and effective. The discomfort you feel with simplification is the point. Overcome it.

Assuming the product sells itself. Great products do not automatically find customers. The history of technology is littered with superior products that lost to inferior ones with better marketing: Betamax to VHS, OS/2 to Windows, countless others. "If we build it, they will come" is a fantasy. Building and selling are separate skills that require separate effort.

Copying competitor marketing. If your innovation is genuinely different, your marketing should be too. Copying the language and positioning of competitors puts you in their frame, competing on their terms. Category creators (as discussed in Chapter 12) must define their own vocabulary.

Marketing to yourself. Engineers often create marketing that would appeal to engineers. This works if your customers are engineers. It fails if they're not. The features you find exciting may bore your customers. The benefits they care about may seem trivial to you. Marketing requires understanding *their* perspective, not projecting yours.

The Sequence Matters

This book is called *Build First, Market Later* for a reason. The sequence is the message.

Build first because you cannot market what doesn't exist. You cannot validate a vision with focus groups. You cannot A/B test your way to the laser. The building must come first, protected from premature market feedback that would kill it.

Market later because eventually you must. An innovation that nobody knows about helps nobody. The engineer who refuses to engage with marketing out of some sense of purity is not principled but negligent. If you've built something valuable, you have an obligation to help the world understand it.

The keyword is "later," not "never."

Ludicrous Mode without genuine acceleration is just a button.

Dyson's clear bin without cyclone technology is just a window onto mediocrity. The IKEA effect without functional furniture is just frustration. Perception must be grounded in substance. But the substance that nobody perceives is just an invention sitting in a lab.

Build first. Then help the world see what you've built.

That leaves only one question: Will you give yourself permission to do both? To build something real, and then to stand behind it publicly?

That permission is the subject of our final chapter.

References

1. Sutherland, R. (2019). Alchemy: The Dark Art and Curious Science of Creating Magic in Brands, Business, and Life. William Morrow.
2. Thiel, P., & Masters, B. (2014). Zero to One: Notes on Startups, or How to Build the Future. Crown Business.
3. Norton, M. I., Mochon, D., & Ariely, D. (2012). "The IKEA Effect: When Labor Leads to Love." Journal of Consumer Psychology, 22(3), 453–460.
4. Vance, A. (2015). Elon Musk: Tesla, SpaceX, and the Quest for a Fantastic Future. Ecco.

CHAPTER 15

PERMISSION TO BUILD

The Journey We've Taken

We began in Stockholm, with a question that cut through years of innovation theater: "How can I actually make innovation happen?"

Not "How can I run better sprints?" Not "How can I validate faster?"

Just: How can I build something that matters?

⚠ IMPORTANT

Permission to build is not permission to ignore physics. If you build against the laws of thermodynamics, you will fail. If you build a solution for a problem that doesn't exist, you will fail. Use First Principles (Chapter 4) as your guardrail. Build First means building on solid physical and logical foundations, not building blindly.

Fourteen chapters later, you have your answer. Not the answer the innovation establishment wants you to hear. Not the answer that sells consulting engagements or fills accelerator cohorts. But the answer that actually works.

You learned that innovation theater isn't just ineffective, it's actively harmful. You discovered that solutions seeking problems isn't a bug, it's a feature. You understood why customers can't request revolutions. You saw how first-principles thinking beats best practices. You recognized that systems create more value than products. You learned that technical excellence beats market timing. You discovered the bootstrap advantage. You mastered the Technology Readiness Pipeline. You understood why persistence beats pivoting. You learned to create categories, not serve markets.

The Empty Chair

We started this journey in a Stockholm warehouse in 2013, watching an innovation theater. If we walked back into that room today, the sticky notes would still be there. The evangelists would still be preaching validation.

But you wouldn't be there.

You would be back in your lab, your garage, or your office, building. You have left the theater to do the work.

The Recipe Paradox

Throughout this book, I've shared frameworks, principles, and patterns: the Technology Readiness Pipeline, the bootstrap philosophy, constraint innovation, and category creation.

But here's the paradox that Peter Thiel understood: the moment you follow a recipe, you're competing with everyone else following the same recipe.

This is the crucial distinction:

Following a recipe makes you a good cook. You can execute well, serve satisfying meals, and run a successful restaurant. There's nothing wrong with this. The world needs good cooks. Most successful businesses are good cooks following proven recipes.

Creating your own recipe makes you a great chef. You define what the dish should be. You create experiences that didn't exist. You don't compete because there's no competition for something only you can make.

Every transformative innovation came from someone who learned the existing recipes, understood why they existed, and then deliberately broke them. Elon Musk learned traditional aerospace, then ignored it to build reusable rockets. Steve Jobs understood computer industry conventions, then violated them with closed systems. Chad Laurans had all eight HBS professors advise against SimpliSafe, then bootstrapped to a billion-dollar exit. Jan Koum understood Silicon Valley's growth playbook, then built one of history's most capital-efficient companies.

They weren't ignorant of the recipes. They were transcending them.

What follows is not another framework. It's the opposite: permission to stop following recipes. Permission to build what needs to exist. This is the most important thing I can offer: not instructions, but liberation.

The Permission Stack

What you really need isn't another methodology. It's permission. Permission I'm not qualified to give but will offer anyway, because someone needs to:

✓ Permission to build without validation

You have permission to build something nobody asked for. Every breakthrough innovation started this way because customers can't validate markets that don't yet exist. But "build without validation" doesn't mean "build without users in mind"; it means validate physics before validating markets, prove the breakthrough works, then make it delightful. The permission is to build the capability first, not to ignore users forever.

✓ Permission to take the time it actually takes

Not the timeline VCs want. Not arbitrary sprint cycles. The actual time required for the physics to work, the system to stabilize, and the technology to mature. Boston Dynamics took 27 years. ASML took 20 years. These aren't failures of execution; they're honest timelines for hard problems.

✓ Permission to ignore advice from those who haven't built what you're building

VCs who've never created technology. Consultants who've never shipped products. Coaches who've never faced your constraints. Ignore this book when it doesn't match your reality. The only validation that matters is whether your technology works and whether it solves a real problem. Everything else is opinion.

✓ Permission to bootstrap and maintain control

Despite what accelerators teach, 94% of billion-dollar entrepreneurs succeeded without early venture capital. Customer revenue is better than investor revenue. Constraints force innovation that capital prevents. Building slowly with your own resources isn't failure, it's freedom.

✓ Permission to pursue technical excellence over speed

The venture capital world rewards rapid scaling of mediocre solutions. But the innovations that last come from patient pursuit of technical excellence. WhatsApp dominated with elegant simplicity. SQLite powers billions of devices with a small team. Technical excellence creates moats that marketing can't match.

✓ Permission to create new categories, not compete in old ones

You have permission to build something that doesn't fit existing categories. Something that requires new vocabulary, new metrics, new mental models. You don't need to compete in markets that exist. You can create markets that should exist.

✓ Permission to trust your engineering instincts

Your technical intuition was developed over years of understanding how systems actually work. That intuition is more valuable than any number of customer interviews or market analyses. Trust it.

Permission in the AI Age

In the AI age, you need additional permissions, not to avoid AI, but to use it without being used by it:

Permission to be inefficient. While others optimize everything with AI, explore what AI can't imagine. Use AI for the 90% that should be efficient. Be deliberately inefficient with the 10% that matters.

Permission to go slow. While AI accelerates everything, some problems require patience. Nuclear reactors can't be A/B tested.

Permission to ignore AI suggestions. Just because AI can generate a thousand options doesn't mean any should be pursued.

Permission to be wrong differently. Everyone using the same AI models will be wrong in the same ways. Being wrong differently becomes valuable.

The real moats in the AI age aren't about having AI; everyone has AI. They're about what humans do that AI cannot: choosing what *not* to optimize, knowing when patterns don't apply, integrating what AI fragments into coherent systems, and persisting when AI suggests pivoting.

In a world where everyone can generate the same thing with the same tools, the only sustainable advantage is building what others can't or won't attempt.

The World That's Possible

Imagine an engineering culture freed from innovation theater.

No more apologizing for taking time to build something real. No more pretending customer feedback drives breakthrough innovation. No more pivoting away from hard problems because they don't show traction in quarterly reviews.

Instead, Engineers build from first-principles. Small teams working in stealth until they have something defensible. Companies pursuing 20-year visions, not 20-day sprints. Organizations that understand the difference between invention and innovation.

We have entered the golden age for real builders. As machines handle the routine work and the world drowns in optimized mediocrity, the ability to build something genuine has never been more scarce or valuable. The hype cycles aren't your competition; they are your distraction. Your advantage isn't just access to tools everyone possesses; it is the judgment to know what *not* to build, and the courage to construct the impossible while everyone else optimizes the probable.

This isn't fantasy. It's happening right now, in Shenzhen workshops, German Mittelstand companies, Nordic deep-tech labs, Silicon Valley garages, where engineers ignore Silicon Valley wisdom.

These builders don't ask permission. They don't wait for validation. They don't pivot at the first sign of resistance.

They build.

Your Marching Orders

Stop asking for permission. The entire innovation establishment is designed to make you doubt your instincts. Trust them.

Start building in stealth. In the AI age, sharing your breakthrough insight too early is dangerous. Build quietly. Launch when defensible.

Embrace constraints as features. You don't need Google's resources. You don't need venture capital. Every constraint forces clarity.

Think in decades, not quarters. Real innovation takes time. While others exhaust themselves pivoting, you make systematic progress toward something that matters.

Choose the impossible. Everyone else is optimizing the possible. The impossible, the breakthrough that has no precedent, that's your domain.

Build systems, not products. Products are features. Platforms are businesses. Systems are legacies.

Trust physics over preferences. When everyone else is running customer interviews, run experiments. When they're validating demand, validate feasibility.

The Builder's Manifesto

We are builders, not talkers.

We trust physics, not opinions.

We create systems, not features.

We solve real problems, not perceived needs.

We measure progress in capabilities, not metrics.

We persist through failure, not pivot from difficulty.

We build in reality, not on canvases.

We seek truth in nature, not validation from markets.

We work in decades, not sprints.

We change the world by building what others say is impossible.

The Question That Matters

The engineer asked how to make innovation happen in his organization.

But that was the wrong question.

The right question, the only question that matters, is this:

What are you going to build?

Not what the market validates. Not what the framework suggests. Not what the customer requests. Not what the investor funds.

What are *you* going to build?

The world is drowning in optimized mediocrity and incremental improvements. It doesn't need another pivot. It doesn't need another feature. It doesn't need another app.

It needs what you, and only you, can build.

The Final Truth

This entire book has been giving you permission to build without permission.

That's paradoxical. Self-defeating. Almost contradictory.

But sometimes, after years of innovation, theater, and

methodology indoctrination, engineers need to hear someone say: "Your instincts were right all along."

You never needed my permission. You never needed anyone's permission.

The engineering mind doesn't need permission. It needs problems. Give it a hard problem, the laws of physics, and time, and it will find solutions. That's what you do. That's who you are.

The fact that you've read this far means you're thoughtful, careful, and deliberate. Those are valuable traits. But they can also become procrastination dressed up as preparation.

So here's the final permission, the only one that matters:

You have permission to stop asking for permission.

Not from VCs. Not from accelerators. Not from this book. Not from me.

The engineers who build breakthrough innovations don't read books about innovation. They're too busy building.

The End of Permission

The innovation establishment will continue running its theater. The hype cycles will continue spinning. New methodologies will emerge. The accelerators will run new cohorts.

None of that matters.

What matters is what you build.

Not what I give you permission to build. Not what customers validate. Not what VCs fund.

What *you* choose to build.

There are no more permissions to grant.

There are no more frameworks to follow.

There is only this:

You're an engineer. You see a problem. You understand the physics. You have the tools.

Build because you can.

Build because it needs to exist.

Build because that's what engineers do.

The warehouse in Stockholm remains in place. The methods have evolved with AI-generated insights. The workshop continues with new props.

But somewhere, an engineer just stopped reading and started building.

Not because they got permission.

Because they stopped asking for it.

Be that engineer.

OFFICIAL PERMISSION TO BUILD

ISSUED TO: _______________________________

(Name of Engineer / Builder)

AUTHORITY: By the power vested in the laws of physics and the imperative of progress, the bearer of this document is hereby granted full and irrevocable permission to:

1. BUILD WITHOUT VALIDATION To create capabilities before markets request them. [Ref: Chapter 3]

2. TRUST PHYSICS OVER PREFERENCES To prioritize what is physically possible over what is currently profitable. [Ref: Chapter 4]

3. TAKE THE TIME IT ACTUALLY TAKES To reject artificial sprint cycles in favor of technical mastery. [Ref: Chapter 11]

4. IGNORE THE "FAIL FAST" DOGMA To persist through technical failure when physics are sound. [Ref: Chapter 2]

5. CREATE CATEGORIES, DO NOT COMPETE To refuse participation in existing market games. [Ref: Chapter 12]

⚠ VOID if you violate the laws of physics or solve problems that do not exist.

SIGNED: _______________________________

(You, the Builder)

WITNESSED BY: Reality

From BUILD FIRST, MARKET LATER: The Engineer's Argument for Breakthrough Innovation

THE COMPLETE INNOVATION LANDSCAPE

This appendix provides clear definitions of key terms used throughout this book. Understanding these distinctions is essential because the innovation industry often conflates fundamentally different types of innovation, applying universal methodologies to contexts where they don't fit.

The Dediu Framework: Novelty, Creation, Invention, and Innovation

The foundational taxonomy we use comes from Horace Dediu, technology analyst and co-founder of Asymco. His framework clarifies four distinct concepts often confused in innovation discussions.

Note on Standard Business Usage: Many business books and MBA programs use "innovation" and "invention" somewhat interchangeably, or define innovation simply as "invention plus commercialization." The Dediu framework provides a more nuanced and rigorous distinction, recognizing that innovation can create breakthrough value through integration, architecture, or business models WITHOUT requiring novel invention. This precision matters because it reveals why innovation methodologies that assume all innovation requires invention (Deep Tech orthodoxy) or can be validated pre-build (Lean Startup orthodoxy) miss entire categories of breakthrough innovation.

The Dediu Framework

Concept	Definition	Protection	Examples
Novelty	Something new	Not protectable	A new idea, an interesting observation, a novel approach that hasn't been tried
Invention	Something new, having potential value through utility	Patents or trade secrets	Transistor, laser, CRISPR gene editing, new pharmaceutical compounds
Creation	Something new and valuable	Copyright or trademark	Art, music, literature, brand identities, designs, films
Innovation	Something new and uniquely useful	Market competition, not legal means	iPhone, AWS, Netflix streaming model

💡 **KEY INSIGHT: Innovation is not always based on invention.**

This last point is crucial: Innovation can exist without invention. This is the central argument of this book.

Important Clarification: Throughout this book, when we say "innovation," we use it as a general term that includes:

1. **Invention-based innovations:** Innovations built on novel inventions (laser applications, mRNA vaccines, CRISPR therapeutics)

2. **Non-invention innovations:** Innovations built through integration, architecture, or business models without new inventions (iPhone, AWS, Tesla)

Both are innovations. The distinction matters because innovation methodologies often assume all innovation requires invention

(Deep Tech orthodoxy) or that all innovation can be validated pre-build (Lean Startup orthodoxy). Understanding that innovation is broader than invention reveals why these methodologies miss entire categories of breakthrough innovation.

Why This Framework Matters for This Book

The Dediu framework reveals why both Lean Startup and Deep Tech methodologies miss entire categories of breakthrough innovation:

Deep Tech orthodoxy says: Innovation requires invention (patents, novel science, PhDs)

Reality: Many transformational innovations are protected by market competition, not patents:

- **iPhone:** No patentable inventions in the original iPhone (all components existed). Innovation came from integration. Market protection through ecosystem and brand.
- **AWS:** No novel computer science. Architectural insight about infrastructure-as-a-service. Market protection through network effects and scale.
- **Tesla Model S:** No fundamental battery or motor inventions (licensed technology). Innovation in integration and manufacturing. Market protection through brand and charging network.

The blind spot: Both frameworks assume innovation must be legally protectable (either through patents for Deep Tech, or through rapid validation for Lean). They miss market-protected innovations that emerge through superior integration, architecture, or execution.

Expanding the Framework: Types of Innovation

Building on Dediu's foundation, this book explores different types of innovation (the general term). The categories below show that innovation can originate from invention, integration, architecture, or business models. Throughout the book, "breakthrough innovation" refers to transformational innovations regardless of whether they're invention-based or not.

Types of Innovation by Origin

Type	Definition	Key Characteristics	Examples	Best Methodology
1. Invention-Based	Innovation built on novel scientific discoveries or technical breakthroughs	Requires new fundamental knowledge; Often patentable; Long timelines (5-20+ years); High technical risk, lower market risk	mRNA vaccines, CRISPR therapeutics, Lithium-ion batteries, Quantum computing	Deep Tech frameworks work well. Lean Startup fails because you can't iterate to a scientific breakthrough.
2. Integration-Based	Combining existing components/ technologies in unprecedented ways	All components exist before you start; Value from combination, not invention; Must build complete system to demonstrate value; Often dismissed as "not innovative"	iPhone (2007), Tesla Model S, Smart home systems	Neither Lean nor Deep Tech fits. Requires complete vision before market can evaluate.
3. Architectural	Creating new structures for how systems/ ecosystems work	Defines how others build; Creates platforms, not products; Value in enabling others; Often open-source or open standards	AWS, Arduino, ROS, Kubernetes, Android	Build First. Can't validate architecture without building it.
4. Business Model	New ways to create, deliver, or capture value	Technology may be commodity; Innovation in the "how," not the "what"; Often combines with other types	Netflix streaming, Spotify, Airbnb	Varies. Some can validate, others require category creation.

Innovation by Market Relationship

Strategy	Definition	Characteristics	Examples	Best Methodology
Market-Serving	Creating better solutions for existing, defined markets	Market exists with established needs; Competition is defined; Success = better/faster/cheaper; Customers can evaluate and compare	Most SaaS companies, consumer goods improvements, automotive models	Lean Startup works perfectly. Customers know what they want.
Category-Creating	Defining entirely new product categories where no market previously existed	Must educate market about why category matters; No direct competition (initially); Success = becoming category standard; Customers can't evaluate (nothing to compare)	Salesforce (SaaS), iPhone (smartphone), Tesla (EV luxury), Airbnb (home sharing)	Build First, educate-later. See Chapter 12.

Technology Readiness Context

Approach	Definition	Characteristics	Examples	Why It Works
Science-Push	Innovation driven by new scientific capabilities seeking applications	"We invented this, now what's it good for?"; Technology precedes market understanding; Applications discovered over time; Requires patience and exploration	Laser (20-year application discovery), graphene, quantum computing, mRNA platform	Sometimes you must build the capability before anyone can imagine the applications.
Market-Pull	Innovation driven by known customer problems seeking better solutions	"Customers need this, let's build it"; Market understanding precedes solution; Requirements relatively clear; Validation possible throughout	Most enterprise software, incremental improvements, service innovations	When problems are clear and customers can articulate needs, building to spec works.

This Book's Argument: The market-pull methodology has been universalized to all types of innovation. This book argues that science-push and category-creating innovations require fundamentally different approaches: specifically, the "build first" methodology that lets technical capabilities find their applications.

Common Misconceptions

Misconception	Reality	Evidence
"All Innovation Needs Customer Validation"	Only market-serving innovation in known categories can be validated. Category-creating and science-push innovations create markets that don't exist yet.	Laser, transistor, Internet, iPhone, AWS, Bitcoin: none validated with customers before building.
"Innovation = Invention + Commercialization"	Integration innovations (iPhone, Tesla, AWS) create massive value without novel inventions. Value comes from how components are combined.	Deep Tech orthodoxy dismisses non-invention innovation as "just execution," missing trillion-dollar opportunities.
"Breakthrough Innovation Is Too Risky/Slow/ Expensive"	Bootstrapped companies built 94% of billion-dollar businesses historically. Patient, methodical development often beats VC-funded sprints.	The VC industry needs companies to believe breakthrough innovation requires their capital. History suggests otherwise.
"AI Will Automate Innovation"	AI accelerates invention (generating options) but cannot replace integration insight. Knowing what to build remains human judgment.	Chapter 13 explores this paradox: AI makes invention easier while making integration insight more valuable.

Quick Reference: Terms Used in This Book

Term	Meaning	Methodology Fit
Breakthrough innovation	Transformational (10%) innovation: science-push or category-creating	Build First
Incremental innovation	Core (70%) + Adjacent (20%) innovation: market-serving	Lean Startup, Agile
Deep tech	Invention-based innovation with scientific breakthroughs	Deep Tech frameworks
Integration innovation	Creating systems from existing components (iPhone, Tesla)	Build First
Platform innovation	Architectural innovation enabling ecosystems (AWS, Arduino)	Build First

The Engineering Perspective: Engineers intuitively understand these distinctions. We know when we're optimizing (incremental), when we're integrating (systems), and when we're exploring unknown territory (breakthrough). The innovation industry's frameworks often force us to pretend we're doing one thing when we're actually doing another.

This appendix provides the vocabulary to articulate what you already know.

TRP IMPLEMENTATION TOOLS

This appendix provides practical assessment tools to help teams implement the TRP framework described in Chapter 11. Use these tools to evaluate your readiness to advance between stages and identify potential risks before they become critical problems.

The TRP Readiness Assessment Tool

Before advancing to the next stage of the Technology Readiness Pipeline, use this assessment to ensure you're truly ready.

1. Score each requirement honestly: 0 = Not Started, 1 = Partial, 2 = Complete
2. Each stage has five requirements, so the maximum score is 10 points
3. Items marked "Must have" are non-negotiable; you cannot advance without them, regardless of total score
4. Meet both the minimum score AND mandatory requirements before advancing
5. If you're borderline, default to staying at the current stage; premature advancement is the most common cause of failure

6. Reassess monthly or after major milestones
7. Have someone outside your core team validate your scores; founders consistently overestimate readiness.

Stage Transition	Key Requirements	Minimum Score
Stage 1→2 (Physics to Concept)	☐ Mathematical proof (no physical law violations); ☐ Peer-reviewed paper or validated framework; ☐ Computer simulations showing feasibility; ☐ No fundamental physical barriers; ☐ Clear hypothesis for proof of concept	8/10 (Must have mathematical proof)
Stage 2→3 (Concept to Repeatability)	☐ Physical prototype demonstrates core functionality; ☐ Achieved >70% of theoretical performance; ☐ Data validates predictions within margins; ☐ Key failure modes identified and documented; ☐ Clear path to improve reliability	8/10 (Must have working prototype)
Stage 3→4 (Repeatability to Scalability)	☐ Success rate >80% in controlled conditions; ☐ MTBF measured and improving; ☐ Can demonstrate reliably to external parties; ☐ Core team has deep technical expertise; ☐ No unsolved physics problems remaining	9/10 (Must achieve consistent success)
Stage 4→5 (Scalability to Application)	☐ Cost per unit within 3x of target; ☐ Production rate at pilot scale; ☐ Critical suppliers identified and engaged; ☐ Quality control <5% defect rate; ☐ No fundamental manufacturing barriers	8/10 (Must demonstrate production feasibility)

Stage Transition	Key Requirements	Minimum Score
Stage 5→6 (Application to Market)	☐ 3+ distinct applications validated; ☐ Performance >10x alternatives in one dimension; ☐ Beta users actively using product; ☐ Complete Product Threshold (80%+); ☐ Clear value proposition emerging	9/10 (Must have validated applications)
Stage 6→7 (Market to Dominance)	☐ Paying customers acquired and retained; ☐ Gross margins >50% achieved or path clear; ☐ Sales process repeatable and documented; ☐ Customer acquisition cost sustainable; ☐ Competition cannot easily replicate	8/10 (Must have paying customers)

Warning Signs You're Moving Too Fast

Warning Sign	Risk
Investor pressure for market traction	Building sales infrastructure for unreliable product
Building sales team before repeatability (Stage 3)	Selling something you can't deliver consistently
Raising large rounds on promises, not demonstrations	Commitment to milestones you can't achieve
Multiple "pivots" suggesting technology isn't viable	Chasing markets instead of mastering technology
Comparing to software startups	Wrong iteration speed expectations for hardware/Deep Tech
Parallel development before mastering one location	Replicating processes you haven't mastered
Hiring ahead of capability	Organizational complexity before technology proof
Customer commitments exceeding demonstrated capacity	Over-promising, under-delivering

Signs You're Ready to Advance

Positive Indicator	What It Means
Current stage feels "easy," team getting bored	You've mastered the current challenges
External experts validate without reservations	Objective confirmation of readiness
Can demonstrate reliably to skeptics	Technology works consistently under scrutiny
Current stage constraints limiting progress	Ready for next-level challenges
Team has deep expertise in next stage requirements	Capability to tackle new problems
Success metrics consistently exceed thresholds	Not just meeting, but exceeding requirements
Failure modes well understood and documented	Deep knowledge of what can go wrong
Cost/time estimates based on data, not hope	Realistic planning for next stage

Common Risks by Stage

Stage	Risk	Symptom	Mitigation
1→2	Violates physical laws	No peer validation of physics/ chemistry	Expert review before proceeding
1→2	Unfalsifiable claims	Can't design experiments to test	Redesign approach to be testable
1→2	Simulation-only	No plan for physical validation	Identify smallest physical experiment
2→3	Undocumented process	Only one person can achieve results	Document and cross-train
2→3	Hidden dependencies	Fails in new environments	Test under varied conditions
3→4	Lab vs reality gap	Works in lab, fails in realistic conditions	Test progressively harder conditions
3→4	Key person dependency	Only expert can achieve results	Standardize process, cross-train
3→4	Cost scaling unknown	No manufacturing analysis	Cost modeling at scale
4→5	Cost reduction impossible	Can't reach target cost	Redesign for manufacturing
4→5	Supply chain unavailable	Critical materials scarce	Identify alternatives or vertical integrate
4→5	Quality control failures	>10% defect rate	Root cause analysis, process refinement
5→6	Below Complete Product Threshold	Users can't evaluate properly	Build more complete solution
5→6	Performance insufficient	Not 10x better in any dimension	Focus development or pivot
6→7	Easy to replicate	No technical or business moat	Build deeper advantages
6→7	Customer acquisition too expensive	CAC > LTV	Improve product or find better channel

The Persistence vs. Stubbornness Test

Decision	When to Choose This	Key Indicators
PERSIST	Continue when success is possible and valuable	• Technical progress is steady (even if slow); • Each failure reveals solvable problems; • Problem remains valuable; • Runway exists (financial + personal); • No fundamental constraints changed; • External experts validate direction; • Team morale remains strong
PIVOT	Change direction when technology works but context shifted	• Technical progress stalled 6+ months; • Technology works but solves wrong problem; • Market timing shifted against you; • Discovered better opportunity; • Personal situation changed; • Multiple experts question approach
QUIT	Stop when fundamentals are broken	• Physics/constraints make it impossible; • Problem not valuable enough to justify cost; • Better solutions achieved market lock-in; • Lost belief that makes continuation possible; • Opportunity cost exceeds potential upside; • Required expertise can't be acquired

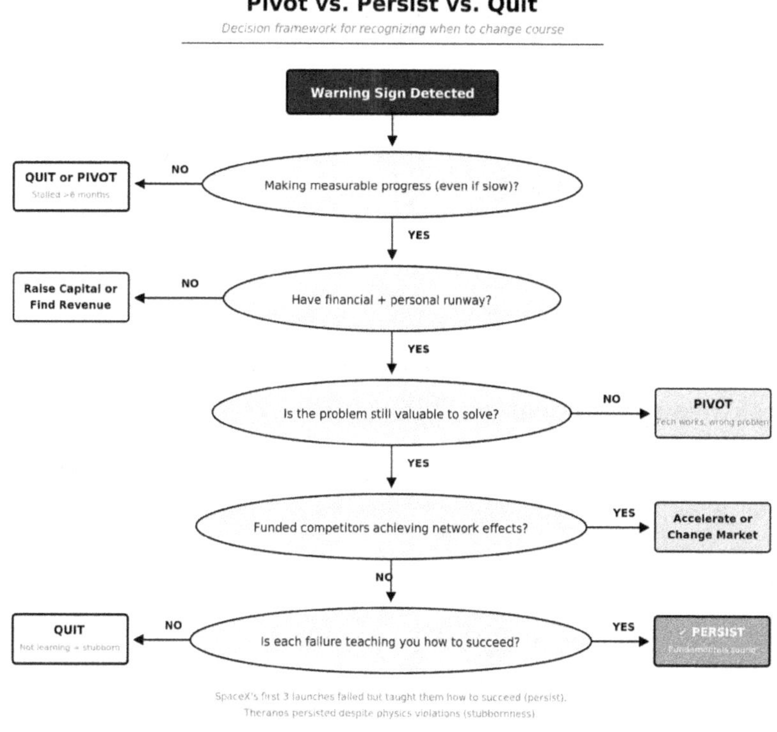

Common Premature Advancement Scenarios

Scenario 1: "The Investor Pressure Pivot"

- Situation: Stage 3 (repeatability at 60%), but investors want market traction
- Risk: Building sales infrastructure for an unreliable product
- Better approach: Achieve Stage 3 mastery (>80%), then advance to Stage 4 (scalability) before market push

Scenario 2: "The Parallel Expansion Trap"

- Situation: Stage 4 (pilot production working), but expanding to multiple facilities
- Risk: Replicating processes you haven't mastered yet

- Better approach: Optimize a single facility to >90% yields before geographic expansion

Scenario 3: "The Vision Over Reality"

- Situation: Stage 2 (concept proven once), but promising next-generation capabilities
- Risk: Committing to features you haven't validated
- Better approach: Master current generation before promising next

Remember: Advancing Prematurely Is the Root Cause of Most Breakthrough Innovation Failures

Better to overachieve at Stage 3 than fail at Stage 5 because you weren't ready.

The pressure to advance comes from:

- Investors wanting to see progress
- Competitors appear to move faster
- Team wants variety and new challenges
- Desire to declare "success" and move on

But breakthrough innovation rewards those who:

- Master each stage completely
- Build unshakeable foundations
- Resist premature advancement
- Accumulate deep expertise that can't be replicated quickly

Use these tools not as rigid gates, but as calibration devices. They help you ask the right questions before advancing, ensuring each stage's work contributes to final success rather than becoming waste.

THE "LUCK" & SERENDIPITY MATRIX

The Engineer's Form of Luck

Between pure luck and strategic positioning lies serendipity: finding valuable things you weren't looking for, through a combination of systematic exploration and prepared recognition.

The word comes from a Persian fairy tale, "The Three Princes of Serendip" (an old name for Sri Lanka), about royal travelers who "were always making discoveries, by accidents and sagacity, of things they were not in quest of." This perfectly captures how breakthrough innovation often happens: you're systematically exploring domain X when discovery Y appears unexpectedly, and your expertise lets you recognize its value.

The Serendipity Pattern in Engineering

True serendipity follows a distinct pattern:

1. **Systematic exploration** (controllable): Actively researching a technical domain
2. **Unexpected finding** (chance): Something unplanned appears during exploration

3. **Prepared recognition** (sagacity): Domain expertise lets you see value others would miss
4. **Deliberate capture** (action): You pursue the unexpected opportunity

This isn't random luck. It's luck multiplied by preparation.

Classic Engineering Serendipities

Post-it Notes: The Failed Adhesive

Spencer Silver at 3M was developing super-strong adhesives when he accidentally created a weak, reusable adhesive. Exactly what he didn't want, in any normal R&D process, this would have been discarded as a failed experiment.

Years later, Art Fry (another 3M scientist) needed bookmarks for his church hymnal that wouldn't damage pages. His knowledge of Silver's "failed" adhesive let him recognize its value for this completely different application.

The pattern: Systematic research (strong adhesives) + accident (weak adhesive instead) + prepared mind (Fry knew about Silver's work) = $1 billion product.

Why it worked: 3M's culture encouraged researchers to pursue "interesting failures." Silver didn't hide his mistake; he shared it widely within 3 M. When Fry encountered his problem years later, the connection was possible because the "failure" was documented and accessible.

Penicillin: The Contaminated Experiment

Alexander Fleming was systematically researching antibacterials when a mold contaminated his petri dish during a vacation in 1928. He could have discarded it as a failed experiment. Most would have. The contamination was an annoyance, a sign of poor sterile technique.

His expertise allowed him to recognize that bacteria died around the contamination. Instead of focusing on his ruined experiment, he investigated why. This observation, combined with his knowledge of antibacterials, led him to isolate the active compound.

The pattern: Systematic research (antibacterials) + accident (mold contamination) + prepared recognition (noticing the bacterial death) + deliberate pursuit = discovery that would save millions of lives.

Why it worked: Fleming had spent years studying antibacterials. His deep domain knowledge meant he could recognize the significance of dead bacteria around the mold. A less experienced researcher might have just seen a contaminated, ruined experiment.

Microwave Oven: The Melted Chocolate Bar

Percy Spencer, working on radar magnetrons for Raytheon in 1945, noticed a chocolate bar had melted in his pocket near the magnetron. This was just an annoying side effect of working with high-power microwave equipment.

His deep knowledge of RF engineering led him to immediately hypothesize that microwaves could cook food. Most engineers would have just been annoyed about the ruined chocolate. Spencer saw an entirely new category of appliance.

The pattern: Systematic work (radar systems) + random observation (melted chocolate) + domain expertise (understanding microwave energy) = invention that changed how the world cooks.

Why it worked: Spencer had spent years working with magnetrons. He understood the physics of microwave energy absorption.

When the chocolate melted, he didn't just see an accident; he saw a testable hypothesis about heating via electromagnetic radiation.

Viagra: The Failed Heart Drug

Pfizer tested the compound UK-92480 for angina (chest pain) in the early 1990s. The drug failed its primary purpose. It didn't help heart patients significantly. Under normal pharmaceutical development, this compound would have been abandoned.

But the drug produced an unexpected side effect that clinical trial participants reported. Researchers' experience with clinical trials led them to recognize commercial potential in what was technically a "failed" drug.

The pattern: Systematic testing (heart medication) + accident (unexpected side effect) + prepared recognition (understanding of what patients value) = blockbuster drug with $2 billion+ annual sales.

Why it worked: Pfizer had systems to capture all side effects during trials, not just intended outcomes. The researchers were prepared to recognize unexpected value because they understood both the physiology and the market.

Vulcanized Rubber: The Accidental Discovery

Charles Goodyear spent years trying to make rubber usable in different temperatures. Natural rubber became brittle in cold and sticky in heat, making it impractical for most applications.

In 1839, he accidentally dropped a mixture of rubber and sulfur onto a hot stove. Instead of melting, it charred like leather, maintaining flexibility. His years of rubber experiments let him recognize this as the breakthrough he'd been seeking, even though it came from an accident.

The pattern: Systematic exploration (rubber treatment methods) + accident (dropped mixture on hot stove) + prepared expertise (years of knowing how rubber behaved) = vulcanization process that launched the modern rubber industry.

Why it worked: Goodyear had tested hundreds of rubber treatments. When the accidental charring occurred, he immediately recognized it as different from all previous failures. His expertise allowed him to replicate and optimize the process.

The Crucial Distinction: Luck vs. Serendipity vs. Strategy

Type	Controllability	Example
Pure Luck	0% controllable	COVID pandemic timing for Moderna: external event, no control possible
Serendipity	50% controllable	Fleming's penicillin: create conditions for discovery, recognize unexpected value
Strategic Positioning	80% controllable	Moderna's decade of mRNA research: deliberate preparation

Pure luck you cannot control. COVID-19, which emerged in 2020, was a fortune for Moderna, a disaster for others. You can't create pandemics or control when technologies become socially acceptable.

Serendipity, you can dramatically increase. Fleming didn't cause the mold contamination, but his systematic research and prepared mind let him recognize its significance. You create the conditions and develop the expertise to spot unexpected opportunities.

Strategic positioning is largely controllable. Moderna deliberately built mRNA platforms for a decade, positioning itself to capitalize on whatever opportunity emerged.

Why Serendipity Matters for Breakthrough Innovation

You can't control whether a pandemic happens (pure luck). But you can dramatically increase serendipity through deliberate practices:

1. Broaden Your Exploration

Dyson's 5,127 prototypes weren't just persistence: each "failure" was an opportunity for serendipitous discovery. Every unexpected result teaches something that might unlock unrelated value.

Practical application: Don't just test for your intended goal. Pay attention to unexpected behaviors, surprising results, and "interesting failures." Document them. Share them with your team. Build a culture where failures are examined, not just discarded.

2. Develop Deep Expertise

Serendipity requires "sagacity": the wisdom to recognize value in unexpected forms. Fleming saw what others would have discarded. Spencer understood what others would have ignored. Domain mastery turns accidents into opportunities.

Practical application: Invest in a fundamental understanding of your domain, not just applied knowledge. Study physics, chemistry, and mathematics. Read outside your immediate specialty. The connections you can make are limited by your knowledge base.

3. Stay Curious Beyond Your Goal

The best serendipities come when exploring adjacent to your target. Post-it Notes emerged because 3M encouraged researchers to pursue "interesting failures." Viagra emerged because Pfizer didn't just discard failed compounds.

Practical application: Don't be rigidly goal-focused. Create slack in your research to follow interesting tangents. Encourage team members to explore adjacent problems. Build systems to capture and share unexpected findings.

4. Create Systematic Conditions

More experiments = more chances for serendipity. More technical capabilities = more ways to recognize unexpected value. Moderna's broad mRNA platform let them recognize the COVID vaccine opportunity instantly.

Practical application: Increase your attempts. Run more experiments. Build more prototypes. Test more configurations. Each iteration is another lottery ticket for serendipitous discovery. But make them systematic; random exploration finds nothing.

5. Build Systems to Capture Accidents

Many accidental discoveries are lost because organizations lack mechanisms to recognize and capture them. The chocolate bar melts, the experiment gets contaminated, the side effect occurs, but nobody notices or documents it.

Practical application: Create systems for documenting unexpected results. Hold regular "interesting failures" meetings. Build a culture where accidents are investigated, not hidden. Make it easy for anyone to flag something unusual for deeper investigation.

The Persian Wisdom Encoded in Serendipity

The original tale of the Three Princes of Serendip offers three lessons:

Be systematic in your exploration (not random wandering): The princes traveled with purpose, observing deliberately. Random experimentation rarely produces serendipity; you need systematic exploration that creates opportunities for accidents to occur.

Stay receptive to the unexpected (not rigidly goal-focused): The princes noticed details others missed because they remained open to surprises. Too much focus on your intended goal blinds you to adjacent opportunities.

Develop the wisdom to recognize value (prepared mind): The princes could interpret clues others couldn't because of their education and training. Prepared expertise turns accidents into insights.

Why Technical Excellence Increases Luck Surface Area

This is why technical excellence increases luck surface area. It creates both strategic positioning AND serendipity opportunities. The more you know, the more "accidents" you can recognize and exploit. The more you build, the more unexpected discoveries emerge.

Fleming's contaminated petri dish appeared by chance. But only Fleming, with years of bacteriology expertise, systematic experimental practice, and openness to unexpected findings, could transform that accident into penicillin.

Serendipity is luck multiplied by preparation.

Every hour spent deepening your expertise is an investment in your ability to recognize serendipitous opportunities when they appear. Every experiment you run is another chance for fortune to favor your prepared mind.

As Louis Pasteur observed: "Chance favors the prepared mind."

Technical excellence is preparation. Systematic exploration is positioning. Serendipity is the reward for both.

Further Reading

1. Roberts, R. M. (1989). Serendipity: Accidental Discoveries in Science. Wiley.
2. Merton, R. K., & Barber, E. (2004). The Travels and Adventures of Serendipity. Princeton University Press.
3. Austin, J. H. (1978). Chase, Chance, and Creativity: The Lucky Art of Novelty. Columbia University Press.
4. Silver, N. (2012). The Signal and the Noise: Why So Many Predictions Fail—But Some Don't. Penguin Press.

SOCIETAL READINESS & CONSTRAINTS

SRL Assessment Tool: When Societal Readiness Matters

Use this framework to determine whether Societal Readiness Level considerations are appropriate for your innovation stage.

Step	Action	Details
Step 1: Identify Innovation Type	Determine SRL relevance	**Socially-Embedded** (energy, transport, urban): HIGH SRL importance **Platform/Infrastructure** (B2B, developer tools): MEDIUM SRL importance **Fundamental Science** (quantum, biotech): LOW SRL importance until application stage
Step 2: Match SRL to TRP Stage	When to focus on SRL	**TRP Stages 1-3**: Do NOT consider SRL. Technical feasibility first **TRP Stage 4**: Begin environmental scanning for societal barriers **TRP Stage 5**: Assess SRL gaps. Where is understanding insufficient? **TRP Stages 6-7**: Actively invest in SRL improvement

Step	Action	Details
Step 3: Evaluate SRL Requirements	Answer these questions	Does deployment require behavioral change? (If no, SRL less critical) Does deployment require regulatory approval with public input? Does deployment affect communities who didn't choose to adopt? Creating new category or competing in existing one?
Warning Signs	Premature SRL Focus	Conducting societal acceptance surveys before technical demonstration Seeking regulatory approval before technology works reliably Building public relations before proof of concept
Sequential Principle	The required order	Technical Readiness → Environmental Readiness → Societal Readiness. Each stage creates foundation for next. Parallel attempts waste resources and create confusion.

ABOUT THE AUTHOR

I am nobody important. Importance has a way of distorting vision.

I'm an engineer who enjoys building things. That's the only credential this book needs.

As engineers, we don't ask who designed a system. We ask if it holds. The bridge doesn't need a famous architect to bear weight. The algorithm doesn't need a celebrated creator to find truth. Function is the only credential that matters.

There are things we only say because someone is there to listen. This book exists because I've sat next to you in those workshops. I've seen your face when they bring out the sticky notes. I've heard your silence when they ask for "radical ideas" while demanding quarterly metrics. These words exist because you exist: the engineer who knows something is deeply wrong but cannot name it in their language.

And there are things that should never be reduced to ordinary words: the moment when impossible burns into inevitable, the elegance of a solution rising from first principles, like water finding its level, the quiet joy of building something that simply works. The innovation industry tries to capture these in frameworks and canvases. They can't. Some truths resist commodification.

Don't judge this book by my credentials. Judge it the way you'd judge any system: by whether it works. Does it name what you've seen? Does it align with reality? Does it give you permission to trust what you already know?

The best ideas don't need famous authors. They only need to be true.

I wrote this for every engineer who has ever sat through innovation theater thinking, "This is nonsense." You weren't wrong. You were the one seeing clearly.

This book is proof that you were never alone.

ACKNOWLEDGMENTS

This book emerged from conversations with engineers, founders, and researchers who trusted their technical instincts despite being told their work wasn't need-driven, but a "solution looking for a problem."

Many of those conversations happened over Swedish fika, coffee breaks, that turned into honest discussions about how innovation actually works.

To those who nodded when I described what was broken: your recognition told me I wasn't alone.

To the thinkers and writers whose work I've built upon, Clayton Christensen's jobs-to-be-done framework, Peter Thiel's contrarian thinking, Steve Blank's customer development (even where I critique its application), and Dileep Rao's research on bootstrapped billion-dollar entrepreneurs, their work gave me language and structure for patterns I had been observing long before I knew how to name them. For as long as I can remember, I have analyzed the world as a system, ideas absorbed from countless books, conversations, and observations until I could no longer trace them to their source. If you recognize traces of your thinking here, thank you.

To the critical readers who pushed back on early drafts: your skepticism made this book rigorous.

Most importantly, to the engineers who will read this and recognize that their skepticism about current methodologies isn't a deficiency; it's discernment. Keep building.

CONTACT & FEEDBACK

This book is written from a systems perspective, and systems improve through exposure to reality.

If your experience contradicts what I've argued here, if you've seen breakthrough innovations follow different paths, encountered failure modes I didn't address, or worked in contexts where this advice is actively wrong, I want to hear from you.

Please share your experiences at: **book@buildwithoutasking.com** or visit **https://buildwithoutasking.com**

In particular, I'm interested in:

- **Counter-examples**: Breakthrough successes that emerged from Lean Startup or Design Thinking
- **Failure stories**: Where building without validation led to waste or dead ends
- **Geographic diversity**: Innovation patterns outside the US, Europe, or China
- **Sector-specific insights**: How these dynamics differ in your industry

This book argues against orthodoxy.
The last thing I want is to replace one rigid framework with another.
Challenge these ideas. Reality should always have the final say.